MAKING IT IN
PHOTOGRAPHY

G. P. PUTNAM'S SONS
NEW YORK

MAKING IT IN
PHOTOGRAPHY

by AMY RENNERT with
photographs by BRUCE CURTIS

Published simultaneously in Canada by
Academic Press Canada Limited, Toronto.
Printed in the United States of America

Library of Congress Cataloging in Publication Data
Rennert, Amy.
    Making it in photography.
    Includes index.
    SUMMARY: Examines the routines and regimens of
professional photographers working in such areas as
sports, travel, and medicine. Also includes a directory of degree and non-degree programs.
    1. Photography—Vocational guidance—Juvenile
literature. [1. Photography—Vocational guidance.
2. Vocational guidance] I. Curtis, Bruce.
II. Title.
TR154.R46   770′.232   79-19099
ISBN 0-399-20691-4

CONTENTS

To Anita, Ellen and Pieter
For being a part of the picture.

To Gussie and Max,
with love.

THE PHOTOGRAPHY EXPLOSION | 1

If a picture is really worth a thousand words, then professional photographers turn out volumes each day as their cameras do the talking by clicking constantly.

Perhaps the saying exists because photography can record with amazing accuracy images of life as they happen. The camera can capture much more than the human eye, and it has the power to zoom in on a single moment in time and separate that moment from all else.

Cameras are used to call attention to events which occur and conditions that exist. Thanks to photography, we can feel as though we were present at the inauguration of John F. Kennedy or we can relive the thrill of Babe Ruth's home runs.

Or we are lured to faraway lands and fabulous places, as pictures stare up at us from the advertising pages of magazines, newspapers and billboards.

Or we are confronted with the reality of poverty, despair, and ugliness.

These days photographs are also being treated and seen as art objects. Galleries devoted exclusively to photography have opened in New York and throughout the country. And numerous other art galleries and museums include photographic exhibits along with paintings and sculpture.

More and more photographers are able to make a living by

selling prints of their photographs to galleries and the public. Twice a year, there are auctions in New York City where photographs and other art pieces are sold to the highest bidders.

Those who wish to pursue a career in photography may choose from a variety of specialized fields. There are food, fashion, travel, industrial, studio, editorial, medical, architectural, and commercial photographers. Photojournalists and photography editors are on staff at every major magazine and newspaper in the country.

Still, you don't have to take pictures to have a career in photography. Maybe you'd prefer to be the owner of a gallery or to be a writer for a photography magazine. Perhaps you'd rather work in the labs developing film, or at a shop fixing broken cameras. And there are hundreds of teachers of photography at universities and schools across the country. The large camera corporations are always looking for employees to keep the business of manufacturing and selling equipment thriving.

Simplified technology enables everyone to make pictures. The word "photography" means "drawing with light." Some of today's compact cameras do everything except point the lens and tell you when to click the shutter. More than half the families in the United States own cameras. Taking pictures is so easy.

And yet, it's so complicated. For the increasing number of people joining the ranks of professional photographers, camera work involves a great deal more than saying "smile" and pushing the shutter button. These people have a tremendous knowledge of darkroom procedures and the other technical aspects of their field.

I don't. If someone were to lock me in a darkroom, I wouldn't have the faintest idea how to go about developing a roll of film to produce tiny visible images. I wouldn't know where to begin in order to make positive photographs, called prints, from negatives, even if the developing process had been completed for me. Enlargers, the different chemical solutions, lights, and processing papers would leave me dumbfounded.

But put me in a room filled with photographers and I wouldn't be at a loss for what to do. All the people I interviewed proved to be fascinating and my art will be to illustrate their stories in words worth a thousand pictures.

In this book I don't attempt to explore all the technical aspects of photography. It's not a how-to-do but rather a how-to-become guide. There are already many books detailing intricacies of the camera. This book examines the routines and regimens of experts, along with their affection for photography.

While most of these professionals got their starts in a darkroom and had little, if any, formal training, they recommend that newcomers to the field get some instruction to learn the basics. They stress the importance of working as an apprentice or assistant to a professional. Most important, they suggest that anyone interested in a career in photography talk to as many professionals as possible to learn what it's all about.

Photographers are often envied by their friends and the general public. After all, they take pictures of all the famous people we see in books, magazines and newspapers. They meet and talk with Presidents, movie stars, rock musicians and other national and international figures. Yes, photography is a glamorous profession.

With the glamour and thrills, however, come long working hours, late night schedules, and deadline pressures. Sometimes there is just too much to do in too little time.

Most of the professionals admit that they have to make sacrifices because of their jobs. But not one of them regrets his career choice or would have it any other way if he could start all over again.

2 | PHOTOJOURNALISM

Whether you live in New York, California, or anywhere in between, there's a good chance you've seen some of Dave Pickoff's photographs. If his name doesn't sound familiar, it's because "AP Wirephoto" usually appears underneath his work.

For twenty-two years, Dave has been a staff photographer for the New York bureau of the Associated Press. His assignments have included such diverse activities as taking pictures of every president since Harry Truman, snapping shots of fires and disaster scenes from miles above the action, covering the race riots in Chicago, and photographing the United States Open tennis championships since 1956.

Dave is in New York by choice. He could have selected any one of the Associated Press bureaus in cities throughout the world. Each bureau has a staff to cover events in a given territory. Every day the reporters and photographers in different areas report the news, which is then distributed to the thousands of newspapers and magazines that subscribe to the AP wire services. News stories, features, and photographs are sent via an electronic newswire to subscribers, where they are selected for publication depending on the individual needs and wants of the various editors.

12 | "There's no profession I'd prefer and no place I'd rather

work," Pickoff says enthusiastically. He's one of seven AP photographers in New York, and one of approximately fifty-six in the country.

"When I first started with AP," he recalled, "I worked whenever and wherever I was needed. Mostly, I covered general late-breaking news items and night sports."

Time and experience have earned Dave the Page One assignments: the presidential elections, the 1976 Democratic convention, the New York blackout, and notorious murder stories like the "Son of Sam." The list is endless.

"The nature of these assignments demands a keen sense of observation and a trained eye," Dave explained. He and other news photographers understand the importance of being able to see "optically."

"Before I even pick up my camera, I view a situation as though I'm peering through the lens," Dave said. "Whenever I have the time, I like to see the subject with my own eyes to help me choose a lens which can achieve the desired effect."

Most of us see a total picture, absorbing numerous visual experiences simultaneously. We are not as selective as a photographer. While Dave can focus on an individual at a political gathering, others do not separate that person from the crowd with such fine precision.

In order to convey a situation or event accurately, Dave never photographs just the sensational aspects. Instead, he tries to capture a myriad of significant details.

"I want the readers to learn from my pictures how something happened. I want them to gain an understanding of a situation, as though they had been at the scene with me. In fact, what I really want is for the readers' comprehension to be greater than the witnesses'."

Often people who observe events live are too caught up in their own emotions to get a true picture. The bride's mother, for instance, may be so wrapped up in thoughts of her daughter's getting married that she doesn't notice the

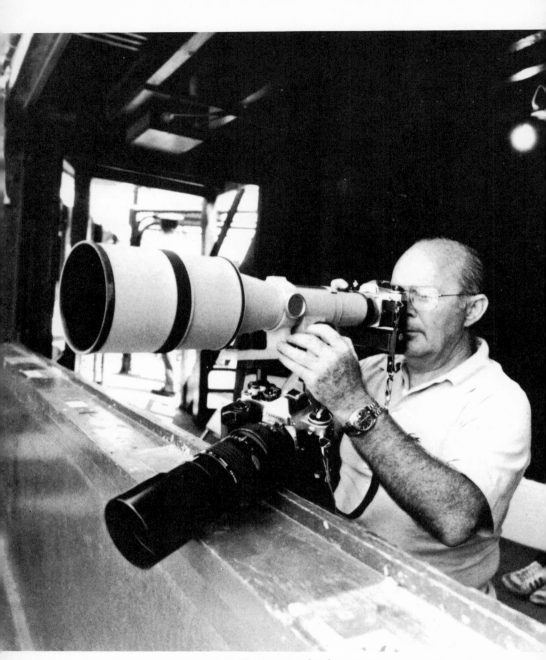

Photojournalist Dave Pickoff adjusting his lens

guests getting restless during the long ceremony. A picture could reflect that mood.

In addition to all the necessary technical skills required for good news photography, an intense curiosity, a yearning to be part of what's happening, and an ability to develop a rapport with people are essential.

For scheduled events, Dave always arrives early. "Over the years, I've found it extremely helpful to build contacts with the police, reporters, politicians and the general public. From them I get insights or learn about attitudes that affect any given situation. Also, many of these people I meet up with time and time again. It would be foolish not to get to know them."

Whenever possible, the AP man will opt for the candid shots. In Dave's opinion, a photograph of Jimmy Carter caught off guard in a moment of reflection is far superior to all those taken when he looks out at the press cameras and smiles as if to say "Okay everybody, shoot."

These days, thanks to technological advancements, it's much easier to take pictures of people without their being aware of the camera. Still, Dave never waits long periods of time for just the right moment. He and other press photographers shoot constantly. During the Democratic convention Dave turned in ten to fifteen rolls of film each day, with thirty-six frames on every roll.

"Whenever any of the candidates moved, I took a picture," he said. "A sneeze, a handshake, a frown—I got it all on film."

His photograph of the Carters and Mondales celebrating the nomination was awarded special recognition.

"I knew it was a winner when I snapped it. I felt I'd captured all their feelings in that single instant."

Photographing leading politicians is obviously nothing new for Dave, but his attitude has changed over the years.

"I can vividly remember my first time being in the same

room with a president. It was when Harry Truman was in office. My heart was beating so fast that I thought it would jump right out of my chest. While the other photographers went about their work looking calm and collected, I barely managed to press the shutter release to take pictures. Slowly, I've grown accustomed to being around the headliners, and now I can honestly say that President Carter's is just another face."

Dave takes his work very seriously. And why shouldn't he? News photographers have a tremendous influence over public opinion. First, they create impressions about people we've never met and places we've never seen. Second, their pictures are observed by millions of people around the world who speak different languages and have different intellectual and political viewpoints.

The advent of the electronic image on the television screen may have scooped the newspaper photographs in recent years, but it has not taken away the need for them. Only the still picture that appears in print can be looked at again and again. Only the still can be referred to at exactly the moment a reader chooses to see it. Printed images can encourage exploration and expansion of vision.

"Because my photographs are so potentially powerful, I'm always careful to be objective. I realize that I'm somewhat selective in my choice of angles, how much background to include and how close up to shoot, but I don't let my feelings about the subject blur or distort my vision. That means I don't just shoot David Berkowitz, the 'Son of Sam' suspect, at moments when he looks hostile or brutal. I try to capture all sides of his character. I consider myself a realist. I'm conscious of my emotions in order not to let them get in my way."

A caption always appears next to Associated Press and other newspaper photos. The words serve to put the picture into its proper context. Together they create a more real

Finished photo of Andrew Young by Dave Pickoff

experience than either could do on its own.

Dave generally doesn't write the captions. When he finishes shooting a roll of film, he makes a notation of what each frame contains and then hands it over to a messenger who takes it to the AP lab for developing and writing captions.

On a number of occasions, Dave has had no messenger available to give his film to and he's been unable to leave the scene because the action is continuing.

"I'll never forget an incident during the race riots in Chicago. I knew the bureau needed my film immediately so that they could start sending pictures out on the wire service. I also knew that it was impossible for me to leave the riots because so much was still happening. So, I took a chance by having faith in a stranger. A guy passed on a motorcycle and I asked him if he'd drop off some film for me at the AP office. I obviously had no way of knowing if the film would ever get there. It did, and I was delighted to find that people can be so trustworthy."

Dave Pickoff could wax eloquent for hours about all the positive experiences he's had since being in the photography business. His enthusiasm is contagious.

"Every day is a new adventure for me. I look forward to waking up early each morning. I rarely know what my assignments for the day will be until I report to work. Generally, I'm on call from 8 A.M. to 5 P.M., though I'm often kept on the job much later into the night. After all, news doesn't stop being made so Dave Pickoff can go home and relax," he said, smiling. "My work is never a chore, always a pleasure. If that ever changes, I'll quit."

Although Dave doesn't develop his own pictures now and, in that sense, differs from many other news photographers, his photography career began in a darkroom.

"When I turned thirteen, my parents gave me a developing kit for my birthday. While other children were outside

playing ball, I was setting up a darkroom in one of our | 19
bathrooms. I just followed the instructions. It was easy. My
parents encouraged me, even though my mother was pretty
nervous about my mixing chemicals in the house.

"After about a year, I started my own little business
developing film for friends and neighbors. I did a good job,
so the business grew."

Dave later chose to attend a school specializing in photography. After finishing, he was fortunate to land a job
assisting photographers on a small Texas newspaper.

"At first, I was just a messenger boy. One day a report
came over the police radio indicating a fire in the neighborhood. None of the staff photographers was available, so the
assignment was given to me.

"I raced out of the office, getting lost on the way to the fire
because I was so nervous. But I finally managed to get there
and take the picture. I must have done a competent job
because ever since, I've been on the streets."

Or he's been up in the air. Dave is the main aerial photographer for the AP in New York. Up in airplanes and helicop-
ters, from a vantage point that would be impossible to
duplicate on the street, he sights and shoots fires, accidents,
and traffic jams. He admitted that shooting from an airplane
was difficult at first, but a good sense of balance and
thorough knowledge of the equipment have made him an
expert at aerial photography.

"After twenty-two years with AP, I feel able to handle any
assignment. My technical training is so complete that my
use of the machine is purely reflex. I've grown accustomed
to reacting quickly.

"But that's not to imply," he added, "that I've got nothing
left to learn. On the contrary, I pick up new skills all the
time. Lately, in fact, I've been spending more and more
time evaluating my work and determining how to make
improvements."

20 | Which goes to show, the smartest person is often the one who knows just how much he doesn't know.

At the same time, Dave Pickoff's pictures are ample proof of all he does know.

FASHION PHOTOGRAPHY | 3

When Leslie Priggen was taking pictures for *Sports Illustrated*, she was given specific instructions as to how to dress for basketball games. In those less liberated days, she was the only woman photographer on the gym floor and there was concern that the former fashion model's shapely figure would be distracting to the players.

That was seven years ago and times have changed. Leslie has left the sports arena to reenter the world of fashion. The only difference is that this time she's on the viewfinder's side of the camera.

"I had tried modeling for a while when I first came to the city, but I found I hated it. But I do enjoy working with models now. I've discovered that they take care of their bodies, eyes and skin in the same way I take care of my studio, equipment, and professional relationships. They invest in their looks while I invest in my business," she says.

Perhaps it is Leslie's understanding of the demands made on models that helps her to work so well with them. She seems to have a knack for getting her subjects to feel comfortable and give a first-rate performance in front of the camera.

Most of Leslie's accounts are art directors who choose her over several hundred other fashion photographers. Having her own representative who travels across the country to

Fashion photographer Leslie Priggen with model and make-up consultant

show her portfolio and tell art directors and advertisers
about her work obviously contributes to her success in
landing these accounts.

The pictures Leslie takes are generally for advertisements
to be featured in newspapers and magazines; most of her
photographs are designed to reveal the appeal of various
fashions and beauty products.

Together, Leslie and the art directors choose models and
design the sets—background, displays, lighting—for different ads. "It's best if it's a cooperative effort," she explains.

Also, since she works with so many models regularly,
she's often asked to decide who has the best hair style for a
certain ad or who has a suitably athletic look. "It's important
that my judgment be trusted, even though I don't have the
final say. Clients always have the last word.

"Over the years, I've learned that it's not a smart move to
argue with an art director, because he's already spent a great
deal of time doing market research and making basic
decisions about how to sell his product. In fact, if someone
comes to me and claims he wants a woman with a purple
nose, I'll do it that way.

"Photographers with big egos who insist on always doing
things their way often wind up losing clients."

Leslie's first big break into fashion photography was when
she landed a major New York department store as a client.
For more than two years she worked almost exclusively for
them doing most of their newspaper ads. Her last year there
was the most satisfying because she received a credit line for
her pictures.

Most photographers who take the fashion pictures we
view daily in the nation's newspapers and magazines remain
anonymous. Leslie got special treatment in reward for
special service.

Photographers whose names regularly appear alongside
their work or in the magazines' staff listings are known as
editorial photographers. Their work is not designed to sell

specific products. Instead it serves to help boost the circulation of the publication.

Leslie has done some editorial work and she enjoys the flavor of it, but she finds the schedule too demanding.

"Most editorial photographers don't have their own studios. Instead they travel constantly to different locations for their shootings. Now that I'm raising a young daughter and working in my own studio, the lifestyle of editorial photographers is not for me."

The majority of Leslie's shootings take place in New York in her upper east side studio. She rents the entire second floor of an older building. There is a reception area, consultation space and, of course, sets where she can do the necessary camera work. Since the studio is her second—and sometimes first—home, Leslie's knowledge of interior lighting has become a great asset.

"I'm not a technical photographer," she explains. "That's not my orientation. My understanding of cameras is not second nature, but something I have to work at. But I'll be the first to admit that I'm terrific with lighting and framing."

Evidently Leslie's lighting techniques are so striking that others in the competitive field of fashion photography are anxious to discover exactly how she achieves the effects she does. Once at a party given in her studio, Leslie caught a rival photographer examining her sets and taking detailed notes. You can bet that guest wasn't invited again.

Looking back, Leslie realizes that her involvement with the department store had its disadvantages. It was her only major account for a long period of time. When she stopped doing its ads, she experienced a difficult few months trying to get new work in order to keep the business alive.

Her success is a tribute to her recognition of the myriad factors involved. "Not only is it important for me to be creative and proficient with the cameras, but also, it's a must that I know how to develop solid working relationships with art directors and others in the business."

Leslie Priggen advising her lighting crew

Leslie explains that each month brings different assignments and, therefore, different money. "In July, I may take in only $2,000 and then in August, I may make as much as $20,000.

"I know that sounds like a huge amount, but I never take all that home in my back pocket. There are expenses to be paid, including rent, equipment costs, and assistants' salaries."

Occasionally Leslie has a morning or afternoon shooting which doesn't bring in a penny. Her only payoff for these sessions is more photographs for her portfolio. But whether Leslie is doing a free shooting or handling a lucrative account doesn't alter her attitude in the studio. She always insists on "getting a good thing going."

She does this best by bringing out the humor in each situation. "Too many photographers are so serious that their fashion work often reflects a pale, dead look. I like to liven things up. If, for instance, a model is having a difficult time walking because of the high-heeled shoes she has to wear, or she is outfitted in a blouse unbuttoned to her navel and is trying to cover up, that's funny, and I try to let the finished shots reveal the humor.

"It wouldn't be right if the only way to create a work of art was through negative emotional input and overtones," she continues. "Here at this studio, we laugh a lot. We have fun and we do a good job."

This vivacious young woman loves telling stories about the aloof models who walk through her doors and then leave two hours later, laughing out loud.

Leslie really gets the chance to let loose during children's shootings. On those days—and others—she may bring her daughter and two dogs to work. "You can bet it doesn't take long to get the kids amused.

"It's rare that a child isn't appealing to me. While most fashion photographers seem to dread working with children, I love the opportunity. This place goes crazy and we all get carried away and have a great time. And, incidentally, we produce some terrific pictures."

During shootings, Leslie is clicking the camera constantly in order not to miss a single expression or move. In one session, she may take as many as eight rolls of film.

When the film returns—usually the day following the shooting—in the form of developed slides, Leslie and her two male assistants use magnifying glasses to determine

which are the best shots. Generally, they are the same shots
which she had a gut feeling for when she took them.

It is rare that Leslie has to redo an assignment for a client.
"It wouldn't be fair to anyone involved for me not to do a top

Finished photo by Leslie Priggen

quality job the first time around, especially since most art directors have to meet deadlines. Mistakes could cost me future jobs and, as far as I'm concerned, there's no reason for that to happen."

Nor is there ever a need to get overwrought if things don't go exactly as planned. Unlike some fashion photographers who find themselves shouting at models and assistants when problems arise, Leslie knows how to keep her cool. She can't imagine ever going into a tirade. That's not the way she operates.

Five years from now Leslie's name may no longer be associated with the field of fashion photography. She hopes to move into the filmmaking world to produce features and documentaries. Already she has some filming experience under her belt, having made several television commercials.

Wherever she is and whatever she's doing, one thing is certain: her drive and talent—and sense of humor—should all help lead her to further success.

SPORTS PHOTOGRAPHY | 4

He was out of the house by 8 A.M., and he didn't return home until midnight. Less than eight hours later, he was back on the road again.

For sports photographer Bruce Curtis such long working hours are the norm. Five hectic days of shooting championship tennis, a week mounting cameras on masts during yacht racing, and staying up all night in the Philippines in order to shoot a 3 A.M. fight are just some of the rigors he's endured for *Sports Illustrated* magazine during recent years.

Besides the on-the-spot coverage of major sporting events like tennis, football, basketball, etc., he's developed a host of film features. He spent a week with two leading skateboarders as they traversed difficult routes across the country, and he thoroughly enjoyed a trip rafting down a river in Vermont.

In addition to the work he does for *Sports Illustrated,* the thirty-three-year-old photographer freelances for other magazines, and produces advertisements and prints for commercials, businesses and advertising firms. He's illustrated several books, too, including the one you're reading right now.

"My schedule may be hectic, but I love it," said the energetic cameraman who usually can't remember all the places he's been to in any two week stretch. "I wouldn't | 29 change places with anyone. I like having the adrenaline pumping continuously—before, during, and after every assignment."

Like an athlete, Bruce puts in rigorous preparation for a sporting event. He acquaints himself with the different personalities involved, while learning their strengths and weaknesses. He thoroughly reviews the rules of the game (if he hasn't memorized them completely already), checks out the weather conditions and notes any special circumstances.

"A total understanding of a sport and the ability to anticipate the action are just as essential for the good sports shooter as his camera and equipment are.

"Specifically, I have to know how Connors thinks and moves on the tennis court in order to be ready for his devastating return of serve or his rushing the net."

Bruce always attempts to catch the action at its "peak"; the point where the action has reached its vertical limit. The trained eye can detect the exact moment and take the picture before the downward motion begins.

"Timing must be perfect," Bruce explained. "I've developed a fine sense of timing so I don't miss out on the best pictures."

As for anticipation, Bruce admitted to seeking help from the athletes before game time so that he could gain insight into a player's moves. Whenever he got the chance, he talked to Connors before one of Connor's matches.

Imagine getting to know and talk with the world's top athletes. It's a *must* for any good sports photographer.

"People automatically assume that my home is filled with thousands of autographs, but the truth is I've never asked for one signature—at least not for myself. I don't get star struck. Sure, I'm friendly with several of the athletes, but maintaining a business relationship is what really counts."

Still, even Bruce has heroes and favorites in any competition. He just doesn't let personal biases influence his photography.

has familiarized himself with all he needs to know. He's also made the necessary technical decisions about which lens to start with and how much depth of field (the area in front of and behind the subject of the picture which is in a sharp focus) to achieve.

Usually the five-foot-five photojournalist is saddled with three heavy camera bags containing five Nikon motorized cameras, light meters, and numerous lenses. Each of the cameras is exactly like the others. There are two reasons why Bruce needs all of them.

"First, I don't want to have to go home because a camera breaks down or jams. I have to be ready for that to occur. Second, I need to be able to switch lenses quickly so I keep each camera equipped with a different lens," he explained.

If Bruce wants to get a shot of one of the world's top tennis players, John McEnroe, serving, he uses a long tele-photo lens. For a close-up of the athlete with sweat pouring down his face, he chooses a short lens. To get the entire stadium within view, he needs a wide-angle lens.

During an event, Bruce takes many more pictures than those which will be used for publication. He's constantly clicking away to produce thousands of pictures out of which maybe ten will reach the printed page. He claims to have a sixth sense about which shots will be the headliners.

"I tend to remember the special clicks. A prime example is the 1977 United States Open. The finals pitted Argentina's Guillermo Vilas against defending champion Jimmy Connors. When the umpire declared Vilas the victor, a roar erupted from the crowd creating total chaos. Fans stormed onto the court and Vilas was lifted into the air. I was being pushed back and forth but somehow I managed to follow Vilas with my viewfinder and catch him as he was at his peak with an expression of total ecstasy."

The following week that very picture was seen by millions of *Sports Illustrated* readers.

Sports photographer Bruce Curtis at the U.S. Open Tennis Championships

all—that Bruce took during his five days at the tennis championships? Many of them have been kept on file with the magazine for future use. Some were published by the Avis company for promotional purposes. Avis sponsored the men's singles at the tennis championships, which means it put up the expense and prize money in order to advertise and have its name associated with world tennis. The company hired Bruce to take pictures of the men's singles and other events scheduled during the tournament.

Bruce keeps other pictures in his files to be used later to interest book publishers and magazine editors. He developed some prints for friends. But the majority of pictures remained in Bruce's darkroom, never having made it from the contact sheet to individual prints. (A contact sheet shows the 36 frames he took on a roll of film in tiny images.)

His first day at the 1977 tennis championships in Forest Hills began at 9 A.M. He arrived at the stadium to photograph New York Times and Daily News staffers playing other east coast journalists in a press tournament sponsored by Avis.

At noon he joined about 100 sports photographers alongside center court for the best matches of the day. After the first men's singles match, Bruce took a quick lunch break with the notorious broadcaster Howard Cosell and tennis superstar Arthur Ashe. They guessed at the individual player's chances, talked about newcomers to the event, and reminisced about old times.

Then he took a few minutes to check in at the other courts for possible photographs of the less renowned competitors. When he returned to the center court in the stadium, there was a mixed doubles match featuring Billie Jean King and Vitas Gerulaitis, in progress. At times, the crowd cheered wildly; at other times, it was so quiet that the only sound to be heard was cameras clicking away, each with its own unique whir or swish.

The camera sounds and picture-taking talk were a distraction to at least one player, who later commented, "It's hard to concentrate when I can hear cameramen whispering . . . 'what kind of lens do you use now?' or 'I only have one roll of film left, what am I going to do?' "

At the conclusion of the mixed doubles, two more players were ushered onto the court, then another two, followed by four more. Bruce remained taking pictures there until the afternoon session was over.

Afterwards he attended a reception and light buffet held under a party tent near the stadium. The dinner was given by Avis for its clients from IBM and other corporations who had come to the tennis matches. Bruce was there to take their pictures.

Snapping candid shots of the guests talking and eating, Bruce managed to do a little bit of both himself before the evening matches got underway.

From 7:30 until 10:30 P.M., Bruce's cameras recorded the winning shots and the big points of the champion players.

On this particular night, the cameraman stayed around Forest Hills talking with reporters, photographers, and players until midnight. Then he drove back to his home on Long Island.

He returned home with the film he had taken for Avis, but he didn't start the developing process that night. Instead he went to sleep immediately so he could be mentally alert for the next few days of action.

With a little variation, those days were filled with more of the same. He photographed Bjorn Borg, Chris Evert, and the new sensation from California, Tracy Austin. He got shots of them on and off the court, alone and with friends, elated and downcast. For Avis, he covered other dinner parties, special tournaments, and award presentations.

After the finals he was probably as exhausted as Vilas. He was ready to put the cameras out of reach and sight for the

Finished photo of Billie Jean King by Bruce Curtis

next few days. Fortunately, the nature of his work enabled him to do just that.

"During assignments, I work my schedule around game time. When I'm developing, I determine my own hours.

Sometimes I work in the morning, sometimes late at night."

He spent two days after the tennis finals developing film and making contact sheets. Bruce circled what he considered his best pictures and brought them to the art director at Avis. The company selected about 300 pictures for its files and publications.

Back in the darkroom, Bruce and his assistant, Waldeen Ozawa, enlarged those 300 images into full-size pictures. After putting on the finishing touches, they delivered them to Avis.

Obviously not all sports photographers keep the same hours and perform the same functions as Bruce does. For example, a cameraperson covering the 1977 U.S. Open Tennis Championships for a daily newspaper in Philadelphia did not spend as much time concentrating on the center court action. In addition to needing pictures of the biggest tennis stars he was responsible for getting shots of the players from Philadelphia and neighboring areas. He sent his film to the paper each night so his pictures could be used for publication the following day. The day after the tennis matches ended he wasn't in a darkroom as Bruce was. Instead he was back in Philadephia recording strikes and home runs at a baseball game.

Although Bruce knows some of the photographers based at small publications throughout the country, he's most friendly with the photographers working for the major national and international publications. He sees them constantly at sporting events all over the world. The smaller dailies and weeklies use the wire services for those events.

There are times when Bruce is the only photographer taking pictures, with the exception of a proud parent sporting a Kodak Instamatic. He attends recreational activities and non-credential sports, like fifth grade soccer games, without an assignment from a magazine or book editor. He knows intuitively that he will be able to interest editors in these photographs later.

The inquisitive creative being within Bruce derives just as much pleasure from photographing a young toddler on a giant slide as from taking pictures of Reggie Jackson at bat.

People all want to know Bruce's most exciting assignment.

"It's hard to say. Different elements make an event a thriller. Always, there's something different to make the work a challenge for me," he explained.

"The Billie Jean King–Bobby Riggs battle of the sexes on the Houston Astrodome tennis court was probably one of the best. There was a sellout crowd and millions of others were tuned into their TV screens watching the brilliant performances of the stars and waiting to catch a glimpse of the victor. I was there recording the moments for those who missed the live action and for the people there who wanted a picture or two to remember the event by.

"Certainly I'll never forget being up all night for the 3 A.M. fight between Muhammad Ali and Joe Fraser held in the Philippines. The bout was held at that time so it could be televised live earlier in the evening in the United States. Within moments after Ali had delivered the final punches, I was on a 747 winging my way back to New York with the pictures I had taken."

As for scary, challenging assignments, nothing compares to the time *Sport* magazine asked Bruce to shoot Kareem Abdul-Jabbar during a practice session. Bruce is afraid of heights, but proved he will do anything for a good picture. He climbed a ladder and perched himself on top of the backboard to take some striking photos of the basketball star.

One thought ran through Bruce's mind at the time: "He's going to leap up and stuff me."

The assignment from *Sport* also required Bruce to shoot an aerial view of Milwaukee, Wisconsin. He had to step out on a catwalk atop a downtown building. Somehow, he managed to get the nerve to shoot the picture which later appeared on the magazine's cover in February 1976. Looking back, the dangers were all worth it. Although, at the time, he wasn't so sure.

Amazingly, the "King," as he sometimes refers to himself, never took a photography course or lesson in developing pictures. He taught himself through reading, observing, and experimenting.

"Until I was 17, photography was just one of several hobbies. Then I started to think that I had a special talent. It seemed my eyes were able to detect much more than the average person's. Over the years, I developed tremendous powers of concentration."

Barely out of high school, Bruce went by boat to cover the

Stroboscope photography by Bruce Curtis

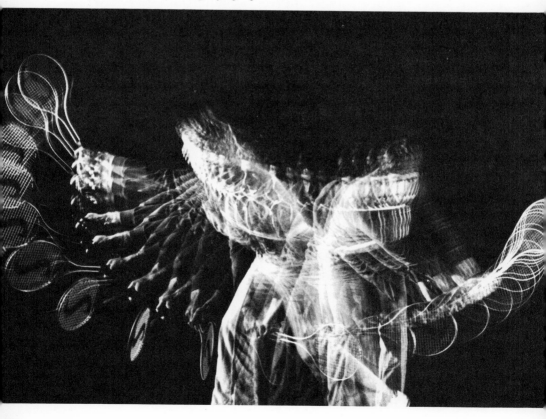

Algerian war in 1961. He did it on a whim, with no backing from any editors. He sent several pictures he took back to the United States via the wire services, hoping they'd be published. Many were.

While away, he managed to maneuver his way inside a terrorist organization and take pictures. He sent those pictures to *Life*, and because of them, was given two years of assignments before returning to the United States.

Bruce took political pictures for *Life* until 1969 when he took his cameras into the sports arena for the first time. He liked the work so much that he's been a sports photographer ever since.

"I suppose the move to sports was inevitable. Athletics have always had a special meaning in my life and action photography has always held the most excitement. I remember my first sports picture published was of Willie Mays sliding into third base."

Bruce mentioned that sports photography didn't really gain worldwide recognition until the late 1960's. Today new specialty picture magazines are hitting the newsstands daily with photos of skateboarding, racquetball, and running. And Bruce has been gaining recognition too. He and two other photographers were chosen by Warner Communications for a national television special documentary on photography, and he was also a guest on a segment of ABC's series "Kids Are People Too." It seems that while Bruce was focusing his camera on some tennis stars at Forest Hills someone else was zooming in on him.

Recently Bruce has been experimenting with the effects of stroboscopes—equipment which produces sequential multiple images in a single frame. If you have ever seen a picture of a tennis player throwing a ball up to serve and it seems as though you're watching him step by step, there's a good chance Bruce took that picture. He considers himself one of the first to work with the strobes—a technique now being widely explored.

When he's not taking his own pictures, Bruce can some-times be found in the classroom at C. W. Post College in Old Westbury, Long Island, where he teaches a course in photojournalism once a week.

If he's not near a camera at all, then Bruce is probably relaxing with friends in his secluded Vermont cabin. Even then photography is obviously in his mind because when he peers out the window to check the weather he's been overheard saying, "Hmm, it looks like an F-8 at 500 day."

MEDICAL PHOTOGRAPHY | 5

As a medical illustrator, my primary dedication will be to the advancement of the medical profession and its teaching program. I will aim in my illustrations to reveal clearly the truth with the fidelity of the scientist and with the sober imagination of the artist. I will avoid plagiarism and I will give credit wherever and whenever it is due.

I will abhor professional jealousies. I will gladly exchange ideas with other members of my profession. I will do all in my power to become a loyal member of my employer's group and I will promise not to breach the confidence of my employer or his patient.

Nicholas V. Levycky signed that statement, had it framed and displayed it on his office wall. The words are a constant reminder of his growing role in the world of medicine.

However, he doesn't get to spend much time in his office reading the statement. As director of the Department of Medical Illustration and Photography at the Nassau Medical Center in New York, he's too busy out on the floor using his camera or his sketch pad to benefit the lives of patients, doctors, and medical students.

"I prepare model illustrations, signs, posters and instructional aids of every description," Nicholas says. "They are used in publications, scientific exhibits, and the classroom."

Pictures serve as visual notes for doctors, because unlike

the actual stages of an illness, photos can be referred to repeatedly throughout the course of treatment. When taken during the diagnostic stage, they help chronicle the progression of disease, or more hopefully, recuperation.

For Nicholas, no two days at the hospital are exactly alike. His schedule depends, to a large extent, on what's going on in the rest of the hospital.

One winter day begins with an early morning assignment to photograph a female patient with an eye abnormality. He checks in with the nurse on duty, loads his camera, and enters the woman's room.

Exchanging only a few words with her, Nicholas takes the necessary pictures and then leaves. Afterwards, in the privacy of his office, he explains this behavior.

"Unlike most photographers, I don't try to establish a relationship with the people I photograph. It just wouldn't be wise, because these patients have ailments or diseases which they are naturally curious to understand more fully. I am not qualified to answer their questions, so it's best if I keep our encounters brief and strictly to business."

Nicholas turns the film over to a lab technician for color developing and begins a new assignment. Using a compound microscope with camera attachments, Nicholas now photographs slides of normal and abnormal cell growth. The prepared slides are thinner than those used for general observation. In the future, these developed slides will be called photomicrographs and viewed in medical classes and conferences.

Next on the day's calendar is a trip to the autopsy department. Here Nicholas uses a special piece of equipment known as a movable specimen box to photograph various pathological specimens. He intends to present these slides with a paper at a medical lecture the following week.

As he breaks for coffee, Nicholas is interrupted by a phone call from the operating room. His services are required

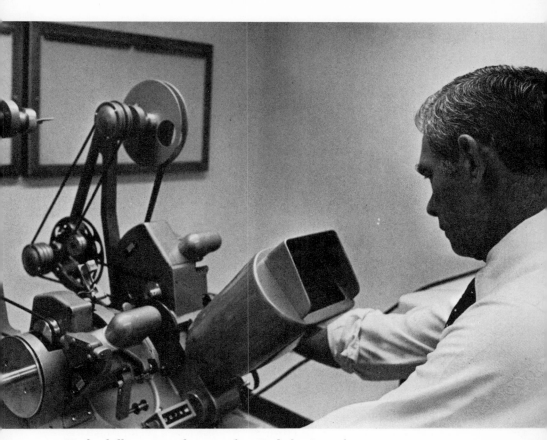

Medical illustrator-photographer Nicholas Levycky

immediately, so the illustrator-photographer hurries off to change to sterile clothing, grabbing his sketch pad on the way. In the operating room he rapidly draws the surgical procedure. Later in the week he will return to fill in the exact details on the rough drafts which he sketches out now. For the moment, it is enough to capture the general scene in the operating room.

This is one of those instances when being a good cameraman is not enough. "It's impossible for a surgeon engaged in a kidney stone removal to open up the kidney and reveal the stone for a camera, so a pen and pad are the means for achieving graphic representation.

"There are times, too, when blood clouds the areas I'd hoped to depict. In those situations I work with X rays and the surgeon's descriptions to sketch the procedure accurately."

During his lunch hour (or half-hour), Nicholas is greeted by many of the doctors and nurses who have come to know him and recognize his work over the years. A physician may stop him to discuss the graphic possibilities of a detailed

Nicholas Levycky

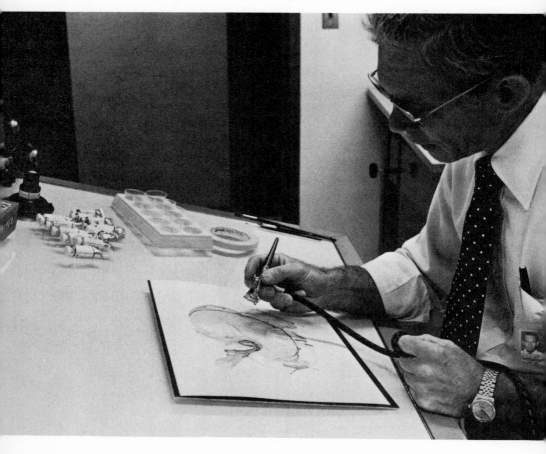

anatomical drawing which will be adapted as a visual aid for a
nursing school program.

Returning to the photography department, Nicholas takes pictures of some of the illustrations completed during the previous weeks. A special Robertson Graphic Arts camera has been designed for this purpose. The prints made are of the finest quality.

Meanwhile, he has turned over an instructional series of pictures for a doctor to use to explain to a wheelchair-bound patient how he can best master the intricacies of the chair. Then a radiologist calls on the phone with a rush order for a sketch of the various structures involved in an X-ray photograph.

At 4:00 P.M. an elderly man with a second-degree burn on his left leg arrives to have pictures taken. Nicholas directs the patient into his studio where he can totally control lighting and framing.

"It's important not to have any distractions show up in the photos, so I use simple backdrops and zoom in on the diseased areas only. I have patients remove any clothing or jewelry surrounding that area."

The final assignment for the day is photographing several different sections of tissues in the mouth. These shots are needed for a unique dental research program being conducted at the center.

Day after day, Nicholas and his staff turn out increasing quantities of high quality work in medical photography and illustration.

Over the years the demand for a medical photographer's talents has risen tremendously and with it the space allotted to the department. In his first year at the hospital back in 1964, Nicholas worked alone in a small basement section of the pathology department. Today he and two assistant photographers and lab technicians have a department of their own on the ground floor of the hospital next to the blood bank and other laboratories. A reception room, an

Nicholas Levycky

administration area, an art studio, darkrooms, photography work areas and a studio are all within the department. Equipment includes contact printers, a variety of cameras, air brushes, microscopes and developing apparatus for black-and-white and color prints and slides. "It's a dream come true," says Nicholas of his present offices.

"Many hospitals, especially in large medical centers, have established similar departments but, unfortunately, most of the smaller hospitals don't have the kind of funds desper-

ately needed for such well-equipped offices," he explains. |
"So·many get started by using some old furniture found in their storerooms and purchasing a few tools. However, a trained and competent illustrator will find these conditions tolerable, to start."

For Nicholas, the decision to pursue medical photography and art as his career was reached during undergraduate studies as a pre-med major. For those who choose to follow his path, a strong medical background is a must.

"A thorough knowledge of anatomy, physiology, and pathology is required since the photographer must be familiar with normal tissues and organs, their functions, and the abnormalities to which they are subject. The muscles, nerves and blood vessels of animals and human beings can be adequately shown or reproduced only by someone who is intimately familiar with them."

Such familiarity doesn't happen overnight. The scientific and artistic training required is offered at several accredited medical art schools including Johns Hopkins University, Massachusetts General Hospital (affiliated with Harvard Medical School and the School of Dental Medicine), the Medical College of Georgia, and the Universities of Illinois, Cincinnati, Texas and Toronto.

Nicholas repeatedly underscores the point that the title of medical photographer implies proficiency in both disciplines. "An accomplished photographer without the necessary medical background can't possibly be successful."

6 | FOOD PHOTOGRAPHY

If you're on a diet to lose weight, then you should avoid ice cream, cake, chocolate soufflés, and Victor Scocozza's scrumptious pictures of all these goodies.

As a food photographer, Victor aims to satisfy his clients by shooting pictures which are so mouth-watering that anyone who sees them can't resist getting the real thing.

"The best food pictures," he says, "capture a mood and involve the viewer. They create an atmosphere that makes the foods far more appetizing and appealing than any straightforward shots could.

"If a housewife looks at a picture I took of butter melting over a bowl of white rice, I want her to think, 'Hey, who wants french fries, anyway? I'll make rice tonight instead.' And a photograph of a thick vegetable soup should tempt viewers even on a hot summer day."

There are several different aspects of food photography, and Victor is involved in them all.

He got his start (and continues to specialize) in shooting for advertisements. Manufacturers, like General Foods, hire him to take pictures to promote their products. It is their job, not Victor's, to arrange for the ads to appear in local and national media. Some of the photographs are

Food photographer Victor Scocozza

enlarged for poster and billboard advertising.

Food manufacturers also turn to Victor for pictures which will appear on boxes, packages, cans and jars in your neighborhood supermarkets. For instance, Victor captured many of the savory vegetable greens featured on Bird's Eye frozen products. This field is referred to as point-of-sale or display photography.

For all advertising pictures, Victor and an art director get together to plan the layout. Usually the director comes to Victor's studio with preconceived layouts and designs. Victor then tries to execute these ideas with a camera, light and a lens. Sometimes the resulting photographs are exact duplicates of the art director's drawings; sometimes it just can't be done that way, and the director agrees to accept the photographic representation Victor has achieved.

Editorial photography, on the other hand, is free from commercial requirements. Here Victor is at liberty to explore many different approaches and be more creative with the camera.

"If I decide to make a sandwich a foot tall, the editor won't hold me back," he remarks. For a spread in *Seventeen* magazine some time ago, he used sixteen different types of hamburgers, showing many bigger than life-size, loaded with layers of condiments. Other magazines which have utilized his services for food spreads on their pages are *Good Housekeeping* and *Woman's Day*.

Several publications rely on Victor and other food photographers and illustrators for recipe booklets and how-to manuals which show the viewer step-by-step procedures on how to prepare certain dishes.

"Lately, however, art directors have been hiring illustrators for how-to manuals. That's one reason why I don't limit myself to just one area in food photography," he reveals. "This way, when one part of the business is slow, another may be thriving."

The popular photographer is always actively recruiting

new clients. He has a representative in New York and another in Chicago. They approach publications, advertising agencies, and food manufacturers with Victor's impressive portfolio. In the future, Victor hopes to have representatives in other major cities.

Even when he has people scouting for him all over the country, Victor tends to complete most assignments right in his own kitchen. Well, that's not completely true. He does work in a kitchen, but it's not at home.

His offices and studio, occupying the entire ninth floor of an older New York City building, include a well-lit, carefully planned kitchen, complete with sinks, stoves, freezer, refrigerator, and all the necessary foods and utensils. It's possible to prepare elaborate dishes here in less time than it takes the average person to cook a hamburger with french fries—or rice with melted butter—at home.

To accomplish such feats, Victor does not work alone. He has several specialists, the most important being a home economist. She expertly prepares all the foods to be photographed.

According to Victor, the home economist doesn't have to be as familiar with cameras as she is with foods, though there must be an understanding of what a camera can and can't do.

"The home economist can't be oblivious to the fact that the camera has a tendency to distort some foods. Colors, in particular, tend to play tricks on the camera. But it's even more crucial that the home economist knows how to cook and bake anything and everything. For instance, a roast must be cooked just right for a picture. Otherwise it will come out on film looking a garish red or an unappealing grey."

The home economist is also responsible for keeping the kitchen stocked with all the right foods and utensils. And she must keep the room at the proper temperature, so that cake icings won't run and gravies won't congeal.

Sometimes Victor, the home economist and the art

Home economist Mary Jane preparing the food

director can complete an assignment in a couple of hours; sometimes they spend a whole day with a product. It all depends on the general difficulty of the job and on the number of approaches the art director wants to try.

"For instance," Victor explained, "pictures involving pouring of liquids require extra patience and skill. Soups are especially hard to photograph because there's a tendency for them to come out looking too greasy or watery. I just have to experiment with different lighting techniques and use different lenses until the picture is as we like it."

While Victor and his crew don't use any trickery like food coloring dyes or special color filters to make reds redder or to enhance certain dishes, they do try to complement the natural appearance of foods.

"Sometimes we'll spray a little water on vegetables to bring out their natural colors. For dark green vegetables like spinach which tend to photograph too black, we choose the lightest of the batch and the economist tries to bring out a bright green in the way she cooks it.

"Some foods may be harder than others," he adds, "but they're all a challenge because I'm constantly working with all too familiar subjects and trying to present them in a new enticing way.

"I don't believe food photographers can treat their work as routine. When they do, it's time for them to go into another business. Any photographer who says 'I'm satisfied with what I'm doing,' is a fool, because there's always room for improvement and a chance to learn something new."

Victor, who's been a professional photographer for twenty years, is constantly learning and he takes on different kinds of projects whenever given the opportunity. Currently, he's doing the package photos for Corning Ware kitchen products.

"Obviously it's not difficult for me to take a picture of a baking dish or storage container. But it's a real challenge to figure out what foods to prepare in them. Really, it's the casserole or soufflé which gives the utensil character."

Victor doesn't even limit himself to food photography. He does some industrial photography and he loves the change of pace. For this work he goes out into the field to factories all over the country.

He recommends that anyone interested in food or still-life photography start by getting the necessary schooling in the technology of photography.

"Besides the general education, it's particularly important to understand graphics and lighting. The next step is to work for a studio for a few years. Anyone who thinks he's ready to go out on his own after a year is probably making a big mistake. Before you start your own business you should be completely confident and able to handle any assignment, even if you've developed a specialty."

While many food photographers are interested in the history and lore of food, Victor insists that being a gourmet is not a prerequisite for being a talented photographer in this field.

"I don't have any particular love for food. It's funny, because when I'm working with it, I don't approach my subject thinking, 'This is something I'd like to eat.' Instead, I view it as a job, thinking, 'I've got to make this look as appealing as possible.' I don't relate to it as food."

But even Victor can be vulnerable.

"Chocolate soufflés are my downfall. I just can't resist them. But then, I'd like to meet someone who can."

MAGAZINE PHOTOGRAPHY | 7

If you flip through the pages of *Horizon*, a slick monthly arts magazine, you'll see one top quality photograph after another. For each picture you see, there are dozens of others which were considered but rejected by editors and researchers.

"Ours is a highly visual magazine," explained photography editor Fred Ritchin. "It's an absolute must that we find and use the best pictures for each and every story, while creating a sense of unity from cover to cover and a sense of continuity from one issue to the next."

This is a difficult job for any magazine to undertake. *Horizon* is more than the 100 handsome pages bound together. Each issue is a major production made possible by a dedicated and hardworking staff.

"If the December issue is scheduled to hit the stands in November, we start working on the art and photography for it as soon as we receive copies of the articles and features to be published in it," Fred said.

In the late summer of 1977, for instance, one of the stories that made its way to Fred's desk was all about the life of André Watts, the famous American concert pianist.

"I turned the story over to a photo researcher whose first task was to thoroughly review the text and decide what photographs would ideally accompany it."

Office of Horizon Magazine

According to Fred, who encourages photo researchers to be totally creative and let their imaginations roam and explore all possibilities, pictures can amplify the text or go way beyond it. The ideal picture is one which is both aesthetically pleasing and a point picture. Point pictures illustrate or emphasize a specific aspect of the story.

"After the photo researcher determined what his first choice photos were for the Watts story, his next step was to find them," Fred continued.

Horizon has several sources for its art. The magazine
relies regularly on only six of the hundreds of photo
agencies. There are also thousands of photographers anxious
to have their prints appear in such a high quality publication
and many of them have portfolios on file with Fred. "I'm one
of the few editors in New York who doesn't turn any
photographer away from my office without seeing what he's
got," Fred commented.

Public relations firms and publicity agents also provide
Horizon with pictures of their clients and products.

"In order for photo researchers to do a good job, they
must familiarize themselves with all of these sources and
establish solid working relationships with them," Fred said.

If no one seems to have the "perfect" photo, Fred assigns
a photographer to the story.

The researcher on the Watts feature decided that pictures
of the pianist during his childhood years would enhance the
piece. For those shots, he met with Watts' agent and sorted
through the hundreds of prints in the file.

Then the researcher contacted agencies which specialized
in the arts. He picked out several pictures of Watts performing at concerts in previous years.

"After gathering the pictures, the photo researcher came
to me and we sat down together. I read through the story
again and felt there was still something missing," Fred
recalled.

"I telephoned a photographer I know who specializes in
conductors' and musicians' portraits. I assigned him to shoot
Watts at an upcoming concert at the United Nations. More
specifically, I described the picture I was hoping he could
achieve—Watts at the piano in all his glory and quiet
intensity with fellow musicians in the background.

Fred got exactly what he asked for from the photographer.
The picture was so perfect that Fred recommended it for the
cover photo, and if not for *Close Encounters of the Third
Kind* it would have been. A preview picture of the movie

was awarded top billing; the photograph of Watts was enlarged and used in a full page spread directly opposite the lead of the story.

"Layout is crucial," Fred said. He and the art director spend hours with the pictures and the text figuring out the best way to interrelate them.

"We make use of proportion and position to design a spread that will capture and hold the reader's interest throughout the story. We often use contrasting pictures on the same page—large with small, dark with light. Sometimes we position the pictures to run across the gutter, which is the center seam of the magazine."

Other techniques employed involve cropping pictures or tilting them at unusual angles.

In short, Fred and the art director do whatever has to be done to create a layout which is visually exciting.

Mission accomplished, the next step was to draw a close approximation of what the Watts story and other articles and regular columns would look like. Then, for the final few weeks before the issue was published, Fred, the art director and researchers moved material in and out of the magazine while making last minute changes and cuts.

At the same time, they were well on their way to putting the finishing touches on January's issue and starting to work on stories for February and March.

For Fred, work in the magazine business is exciting, challenging, and draining. By the time Fridays roll around he finds himself nearing a sixty-hour work week instead of the typical forty.

One reason he's had to put in so much time is the magazine's tremendous growth. What came into existence as a hardcover quarterly in 1952 has evolved into a bi-monthly, then into a monthly magazine two years ago.

While the editors can now provide their audience with a

Photo editors at Horizon Magazine

more thorough and continuous coverage of urban issues and the arts, they're also struggling with the expanded demands of an expanded publication.

"Still, we don't have to do the kinds of rush jobs that weeklies like *Time* and *Newsweek* do. For most weeklies, pictures are secondary while getting the news as it breaks is the number one consideration.

"Here at *Horizon*," Fred continued, "we concentrate on our art and reproductions as much as on our news copy. We have many more photo researchers than the weeklies."

Another change in format is that the magazine is now accepting and welcoming advertisers.

"*Horizon* can only continue to produce an expensive magazine on a monthly basis if advertisers help subscribers pay for editorial, production, and postage costs."

Finally, the magazine is now being sold on selected newsstands throughout the country, whereas previously it was available only to subscribers. Therefore, from a pictorial standpoint, its cover must compete with all the other covers. There must be something about the cover photo that makes the onlooker want to purchase *Horizon* more than the other publications on the rack.

"The cover photo relates to one of the more important stories in the issue," Fred explained. "Usually, I'll make three personal recommendations to the art director. He and the managing editor have the final say. We try to vary the subject of our covers from month to month."

Previous cover photos included movie actress and writer Liv Ullmann and the Boston Symphony conductor Seiji Ozawa.

Fred is pleased by the new direction of *Horizon*. The publication is reaching more people now than ever before. He's been on staff for six years.

"I've been a photo researcher, a copy editor, a caption writer, and a general researcher. Photo researchers don't necessarily need to be photographers but they have to have

an artistic sense and a trained eye for knowing what looks
right. Even photo editors sometimes lack field experience although, personally, I find being a photographer helps."

When it's nearing deadline and the editors realize they have to fill a blank space, it's not unusual for Fred to take a few pictures to run in an issue.

Before coming on staff at *Horizon,* Fred worked as a free-lance writer and photographer for several publications. Many of the people he met in business during those earlier years have proven valuable contacts in his present position.

"I would suggest that newcomers to magazine photography start with any job they can get to learn the ropes and to meet the people in the field. There's always time to move up in the business," he said. "Today, I have connections with photographers all over the world."

The magazine is evidence of that. December's issue, the one with the Watts story, reveals pictures of Euro-communist leaders during a summer meeting in Madrid, seven wineries in California, and the Royal Library at Windsor Castle in England.

8 | TEACHING PHOTOGRAPHY

Not all good photographers start clicking away at age six. Arthur Leipzig didn't go near a camera until he was almost twenty-three.

"I grew up with absolutely no interest in photography. I could never understand why some of my buddies chose to be in a darkroom instead of on the streets playing stickball.

"At fourteen, my friends and I started struggling with the complicated task of figuring out what to do with the rest of our lives. I remember the long hours in the library going alphabetically through the different fields. The A's seemed unappealing—accounting, advertising, architecture. The B's were no better. But I never finished my search for the 'right' job because the time came to start earning some money.

"I held a variety of jobs after high school. Then an accident in a glass factory caused me to lose the use of my right hand for fourteen months."

But Arthur turned his injury into an advantage. While waiting for his hand to heal, by chance, he enrolled in an inexpensive course to learn the skills of a darkroom technician.

"During the first two weeks of the course, I did a complete turnabout and made a decision—I chose photography as my profession. To this day, I've never doubted that choice."

And why should he? Today Arthur Leipzig is recognized | by his colleagues as one of the nation's leading photography teachers and as a prominent photographer as well. He's exhibited his prints in numerous museums and his courses at C. W. Post University are crowded with energetic, eager-to-learn-from-Arthur students.

For the students, the learning process begins on day one.

"The first thing I do in a beginners' class is get my pupils in the darkroom working on photograms so they can get a basic understanding and have a successful experience before they even hold a camera," Arthur said.

A photogram is a demonstration of photosensitivity by means of laying opaque material some special photographic paper and then exposing it to sunlight or an enlarger light in order to create a photographic image.

"After working with photograms, the students start taking pictures. Otherwise many would become so lost in the mechanics and technology of photography that they'd get turned off to picture taking," Arthur explained.

Evidently some technical schools which start the fall semester in early September don't permit students to take pictures or work with cameras until mid-November.

Arthur doesn't omit technical discussions about light forms and relationships, different lens speeds, and other important subjects. He just puts a much stronger emphasis on individual expression. He likes best to let his students loose to explore the world around them with their cameras.

The beginners get a sampling of several initial projects. The first assignment is often an indoor portrait, the second an abstract picture, and the third an animal photo.

Often these assignments are completed during field trips. "Students are always amazed to discover that their observations are entirely different from anyone else's as each of us returns to the classroom with our own special impressions and, hence, photographs.

"Field trips are followed by critique sessions so classmates can get reactions from each other. Slowly, students become aware of their strengths and of the approaches which work best for them."

Arthur learned long ago that his main "focus" is the human condition. Consequently, most of his prints show people revealing their emotions and feelings about their situations.

As a teacher, he makes it a point never to encourage students to follow his footsteps. In fact he goes so far as to say, "One Arthur Leipzig is enough." He also keeps his pictures out of sight until late in the year.

"I urge each student to move in his own direction. I remember how a fellow named Jim used to sit disinterested in all class projects and discussions except for those dealing with landscape photography. Instead of reprimanding him, I told Jim to explore his area of interest further and forget other assignments for awhile. His work was brilliant and eventually he was ready and eager to try other projects."

Then, there are the abstract photographers. "These are the students who try to be most creative in their approach. Often, their pictures reveal unrecognizable objects at first glance because of the various light and speed changes employed. I personally don't find these pictures nearly as exciting as realistic shots of people and scenes.

"Twenty years ago I would have rejected these pictures without looking at them twice. But now that I'm teaching, I'm also learning and constantly re-examining attitudes that I used to take for granted.

"Often I'll make a statement in class which leads a student to ask, 'Why?' I have two choices. I can answer, 'Because I'm the teacher and I just said so, that's why,' or I can honestly trace the means for arriving at such a conclusion."

To facilitate this intensive intimacy between students and teacher, Arthur prefers to keep the class size as small as possible. He's managed to hold the number of pupils in each class down to seventeen.

Photography teacher Arthur Leipzig with his students

This desire to limit class size reminds him of another time. "When I first tried to get a job back in 1952, most schools didn't even offer photography classes because there was little, if any, interest in the subject. During my first year at Post, in 1963, I was lucky to have ten students enroll in a course—the only photography course being given. It's incredible how much things have changed."

It certainly is. Today C. W. Post offers several photography classes, including one in photojournalism, each semester. Almost every college and university has at least one course with facilities for developing prints. Many even make majors in photography a possibility.

There are also several technical schools and ongoing workshops and seminars throughout the country.

"I'm not at all sorry I wasn't able to get a job teaching back in 1952," Arthur continued. "I wasn't ready then, because I was still too involved in developing my own style. I would have tried to get students to praise my works, and I'm sure I would have been very mechanical in my teaching methods.

"By 1963, I was ready and eager to be in the classroom. It happened by accident, just like my start in photography, except this time it was a chance meeting, not an injury. My wife was in the supermarket and a professor's wife casually called over to her, 'Hey, do you think Artie would like to teach photography at the university? There's an opening.' My wife knew it was what I had originally wanted and she accepted right then and there."

Obviously most photographers don't join the ranks because of injured limbs or unscheduled meetings. Many of Arthur's former students are now working full-time as photojournalists, fashion photographers, or one of the other professions listed elsewhere in this book. Others continue to pursue photography as a special hobby or part-time job while turning to other careers.

Advanced students of photography, at least the ones in Arthur's classes, develop their professional employment potential by using their learned skills for creative projects. Two years ago one class published *The Poet's Image: The Photographer's Eye*. The group read poems together, then took pictures which they thought best expressed the mood or feeling of the poems. Together they explored various

techniques of image making. Their finished product is the
book, filled with pictures and poems side by side, reflecting
each other.

Some of Arthur's students have had their works exhibited
in local galleries, libraries, and special showings.

"Whenever it can be arranged, I take classes to visit with
famous photographers who are willing to share their ideas
and experiences. These meetings often leave everyone so
turned on that class runs overtime. I, personally, hate to cut
off something creative just because a bell rings so I try to
schedule these sessions in the evening," Arthur explained.

Some photography classes at Post meet at night, others
are for one hour three times a week, and still others are for
an intense three hour session once a week. The scheduling
depends upon the needs of the students and the administration's flexibility.

Taking classes with Arthur this year doesn't guarantee a
job next year, and the teacher lets his students know the
reality of the job market for young new photographers
seeking work.

"It's a highly competitive field and doors are bound to be
shut in the young photographer's face. Some never even get
opened because people in the business are afraid to gamble
on an unknown. But persistence, confidence, and a good
portfolio of one's work should eventually lead to assignments
and work."

Arthur urges students to be patient and find part-time
work while job hunting.

Meanwhile, Arthur is planning to further his own experience and knowledge by taking a trip around the world to
work on another photography project. Any insights he gains
will be passed on to future students.

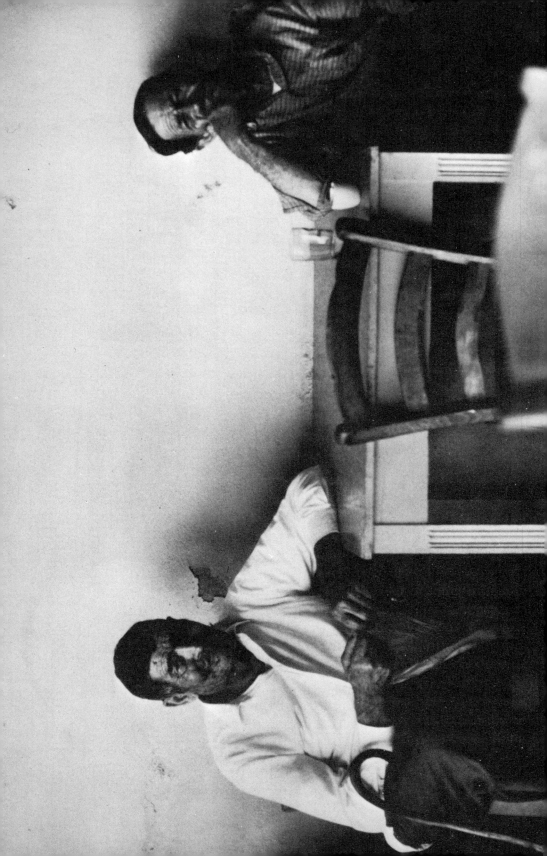

TRAVEL PHOTOGRAPHY | 9

As JoAnne Kalish reminisces about her recent trips to Mexico, Nova Scotia, the British Isles, and Greece, she gets a dreamy look in her eyes. It's almost as though she's been transported back to those faraway shores.

One look at some of the photographs taken during those traveling days and you, too, can drift to foreign lands—even if you've never set foot outside your hometown.

"I make it my business to convey the mood of a country and its people," the twenty-six-year-old photographer explained. "That's why I rarely take any pictures the day I arrive in a new place. First I get familiar with the area and comfortable with the people. Then I load my camera.

"Still, even during my first roll of film, I think of the camera as being empty. It's an exercise of sorts to get my mind working."

No matter where she goes, JoAnne spends a lot of time at cafes, parks, beaches, and in people's homes, where she shares ideas and good times. For JoAnne, people is what photography is all about.

"A photograph of two elderly men getting drunk and laughing with one another at their house (opposite page) reveals so much more than a picture of their home without them in it," she said. The tipsy tipplers referred to were two | 69

Greek men who became good friends during JoAnne's stay on the island of Crete.

She also befriended a local bar owner. "I was there a week. I didn't just observe his life; I became a part of it. We ate meals together, took walks together as he showed me the sights, and relaxed together as he entertained me and his other customers at the bar," she recalled fondly.

Now, more than two years later, she has many wonderful pictures of her Greek host to remind her of the lovely island and of their special friendship. Realize, too, that this man spoke not one word of English and JoAnne had mastered very little Greek. The little she knows was pulled from her constant companion—a Greek phrase book. JoAnne insists that language differences don't have to pose a barrier.

Two of her other photos that are personal favorites reveal a Mexican fisherman—waiting, waiting, waiting for a catch; and a young girl standing in the doorway of her Nova Scotia home looking out to the world.

It's easy to discover which photographs JoAnne likes best. They're the ones which remain on the walls of her Long Island home long after others have come and gone.

Although JoAnne is partial to people pictures, she certainly doesn't avoid using the camera to capture scenic settings. "These pictures usually aren't as meaningful to me and they're not the ones I keep framed in my house, but they're definitely more salable."

And since JoAnne doesn't consider photography merely a hobby, sales are absolutely essential towards pursuing a career as a professional photographer. As a free-lancer, she doesn't get sent to foreign countries on assignment by magazine editors or book publishers. If she did, her airfare, hotels, meals, and other traveling costs would be covered, along with her developing costs. Instead, she pays her own way and does all work on speculation.

"While it's been difficult, as a newcomer, to get actual assignments, I am able to meet with some editors and agents before packing my bags and taking off," JoAnne indicated. "That way I can get some idea of what pictures they're looking for. In turn, they become familiar with my face and my work because I show up at their door with a portfolio of pictures from previous trips."

Obviously it's impossible for the young woman to develop contacts with all the local and national publications, not to mention the thousands of agencies which might be interested in what she has to offer. Furthermore, the ability to take photographs which can sell and the ability to actually sell the pictures are two entirely different talents.

For the selling of her pictures, JoAnne chooses to rely on picture agencies.

These agencies are in constant contact with magazines, newspapers, book publishers, advertising agencies and filming studios, and they keep up-to-date accounts of the going prices. The larger photo agencies, known as stock houses, get requests for new pictures every day.

By using the agencies' services, JoAnne is free to work at what she does best—taking pictures and developing them. She has all the necessary facilities for black-and-white and color developing in her home.

Before JoAnne turns over any photographs to an agency, she establishes a solid business relationship with it. Most of the stock houses take photographs on consignment, which means they take a percentage of the fee a picture sells for. If none of JoAnne's pictures were to be sold by the agency, she wouldn't pay them a penny. On the other hand, if the same picture sells to numerous publications over the years, she pays the agency a commission for each and every sale.

Occasionally agencies try to buy the rights to a photograph before making any sales. In these instances the photographer receives only one payment whether the picture remains in the files or whether it sells a hundred times.

Getting business relationships to work is as crucial to a professional photographer as manipulating a camera.

JoAnne must be cautious when entering into any contracts
or even verbal agreements.

"I always consult with fellow photographers more experienced than myself in order to find out what kinds of problems exist in the marketplace and to keep current with which agencies have the best reputations."

While Leslie Priggen and Victor Scocozza have their own personal agents representing them to art directors and editors across the nation, JoAnne is not yet ready or able to hire someone for this job. Unlike Dave Pickoff and Bruce Curtis, she doesn't have years of experience as a professional. In fact, Pickoff was selling pictures before JoAnne was even born.

As a youngster, JoAnne's interest in photography developed with help from her father. He was a weekend shutterbug the way some dads are armchair quarterbacks.

At nineteen, she took a part-time job with a studio which specialized in high school students' portraits. She remembers staying at work late into the night so she could improve her talents in the darkroom.

For the past three years she has been learning—the hard way—that being taken seriously by agents and editors takes time, dedication, and energy in addition to good work.

"Photographers really have to prove themselves before editors and agents will take time out from their busy schedules to see them," she said. "Sometimes I think it's especially rough being a woman in this field."

According to JoAnne, it's often hard for her to convince editors that she means business and isn't just flirting with a career in photography. Determination, encouragement from family and friends, and technical advice from fellow photographers have contributed to helping her earn the reputation she so desperately wants and is gradually gaining.

Travel photographer JoAnne Kalish

Already she has sold prints to several important publications, including Time-Life's, *Newsday* and *American Way*. Many textbooks and educational periodicals reveal pictures of foreign landscapes JoAnne took during her travels. She's had pictures featured at various galleries and has presented multimedia musical slide shows of her days on the road to students of photography.

One of her goals is to interest *National Geographic* in her work. The publication is one of the most prestigious on the market, with elaborate pictorial layouts of places and people in every corner of the globe.

But she doesn't want to be labeled as a travel photographer only. She's also had several sports and still-life pictures published.

"I love photography, and everything connected with it, and I'm not about to limit myself to just one area," JoAnne asserts. "Not yet, anyway."

CAMERA REPAIR | 10

"Nobody, and I mean nobody, knows cameras like Marty does."
Arthur Leipzig

"If I have a dream and I tell it to Marty, the dream becomes a reality."
Bruce Curtis

"Marty can do anything. He's unbelievable."
JoAnne Kalish

If you don't know and respect Marty Forscher the way these people do, then you're probably not a professional photographer living and working in New York.

Marty plays the role of a doctor. Whenever there's a crisis such as a broken camera having a "relapse" or requiring a "transfusion" or "amputation," Marty has a cure. Over the years he's performed amazing feats of surgery. He just needs to know where it hurts.

Of course, it's not likely he'll be the attending physician these days. What started as a one-man practice has grown to a thirty-person clinic employing some of the nation's most highly skilled camera repair technicians.

It all began in the basement of a camera store back in 1941, soon after his high school graduation. Marty worked in the small repairs department there until he landed a job | 75

Win Moses (right) at the Professional Camera Repair Service shop

with the United States Navy the following year. During the war he served as "Mr. Fix-It" for a group of top photojournalists in the Steichen unit.

"I really knew next to nothing about all the different cameras they used—Leica, Rolleiflex, Contax Medalist,

Speed Graphic—so there was only one thing for me to do in
order not to lose my job," Marty recalls. "I locked myself in a
room and stripped the cameras down to the very last screw.
Then I mixed up all the parts and reassembled them from
scratch. It was like putting together the pieces in a jigsaw
puzzle.

"Slowly, I developed a familiarity with the cameras and
that understanding remains with me to this day."

World War II ended but the need for Marty's services
continued. Many of the professional photographers he
helped during wartime sought Marty's expertise for their
own repair problems.

In February 1946, Marty opened the doors of the Professional Camera Repair Service. His name and reputation
spread quickly as did the number of magazines and newspapers which turned to him for assistance. Magazines like
Look and Life, wire services including the United Press
International (UPI) and Associated Press (AP) zoomed in on
Marty's technical talents.

With so many influential clients focusing on his services,
Marty began hiring employees. The first enlisted, Buddy
Graves, is now one of Marty's right-hand men (and a major
stockholder in the company). The other key staff members
are Win Moses and Willy Keresztes, the shop manager.

As for the rest of the employees at Professional Camera,
Marty says, "Our work force contains representatives of
many ethnic and racial backgrounds. This was a conscious
policy on my part long before it became fashionable, and
time has proven it not only profitable but also rewarding.
The shop is a cross section of the world community, and it's
my belief that this has made a very powerful contribution to
our success."

Unfortunately, there is only one woman currently
employed, but Marty is hopeful that more and more liberated women will seek jobs as camera technicians. He
welcomes their imminent arrival.

The tasks performed by Marty's employees are usually in response to problems not covered in any of the standard repair manuals.

"The simple basic repair, like fixing a broken knob or spring, becomes routine," Marty explains. "But new modifications are always a challenge, calling upon intuition and high skill. These modifications are sought by professionals who constantly push the limitation of their equipment."

Some of the Professional Camera Repairs' out-of-the-ordinary jobs included the development of brackets for a camera to be carried on a bobsled so it could withstand vibrations and gravitational forces at high speeds, mounts for skydiving helmets, and attachments for skis.

One of Marty's most satisfying experiences was designing special equipment for a professional who had broken his right wrist.

"This fellow was in total despair. He thought his career as a photographer had come to an abrupt end. I'm thankful that I was able to help."

Marty's technical genius has even made a critical contribution to the world of medicine. He designed a special-purpose camera that can process film immediately. The camera is similar to the cameras which release a print within minutes after the shutter is clicked. The advantage of the camera Marty designed is that it can take four pictures—one right after another—and develop them immediately, side by side. Doctors are excited by their newfound ability to shoot instant photographs with 35mm single-lens relex cameras. In fact one doctor claimed that the new camera eliminated almost eighty percent of the paper work he used to have in writing up extensive, descriptive medical reports.

One of Marty's most difficult assignments was the conception and development of motor drives for the Leica cameras used to record an aircraft crew flying under battle conditions. The drives were used aboard a non-stop flight of a

B-52 bomber and the pictures were later shown to the world | 79
in *Life* magazine.

"That was a real challenge for us because we worked under the pressure of a strict deadline. We took what was

Repairman at Professional Camera Repair Service shop

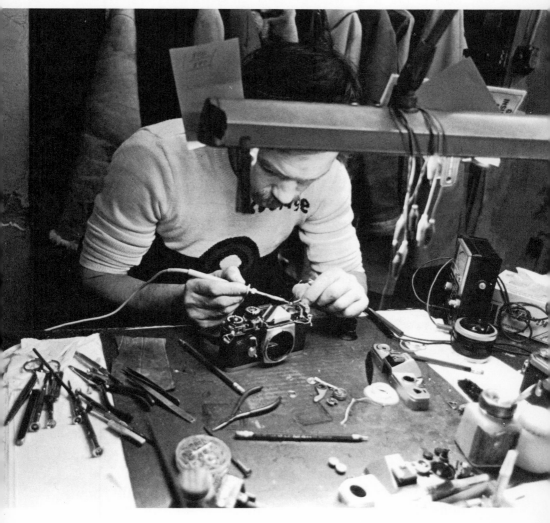

Win Moses (left) with Marty Forscher (right)

available to us in the marketplace and built a workable system in record time."

It's not at all unusual for Marty and the others at the Repair Service to initiate concepts that manufacturers admire and imitate.

Because of the advancements made by his shop, repair
stores in general have developed better relationships with
camera manufacturers.

"In the 1940's the manufacturers were very reluctant to
deal with us. They viewed us as unnecessary competition,"
Marty noted. "But now that we've proved ourselves, there's
an atmosphere of mutual respect. They no longer keep all
technical information secret."

The tremendous advances in cameras and film have
signaled other changes in the world of camera repair.

"Basic mechanical skills are no longer sufficient," Marty
explains. "The new electronics and computer technology in
camera design demand sophisticated skills that probably
ought to be learned in the classroom."

He recommends interested students to also get on-the-
job training as apprentices and look into the National
Camera Technical Training Division, Inc. programs in
Englewood, Colorado.

Marty wants it known that he still prefers working with
the older mechanical cameras which aren't automatic like
the ones manufactured for the general public.

Actually, he's not working with either kind of camera too
much these days because his position at the shop is not what
it used to be. He's assumed the role of administrator which
means he spends most of his time involved in the business.
In this capacity, he's constantly trying to figure out a way to
get more space for his ever-expanding offices at 37 West
47th Street in Manhattan. What started in a small area in the
front corner of the ninth floor has already grown to occupy
the entire floor. Even this long coveted space is proving
inadequate to meet the burgeoning demands placed upon
the shop's unique expertise.

Marty's attitude at work remains unchanged. He continues to concern himself with his customers as well as their
equipment. He's involved in numerous causes outside the

office and he's helped to set up photography programs for several organizations and youth groups.

Two years ago Marty received a fellowship award from the National Press Photographer Association for being "the ultimate problem solver for working photographers" and for "unselfishly giving his knowledge, encouragement, goodwill and unending friendship."

OTHER CAREERS | 11

As wide-ranging as this book has attempted to be, it does not cover all of the possible careers in photography. While many specialty areas have been discussed, several alternative professions remain unexplored. Positions spanning the field from arts to camera parts and from photo detail to selling retail are also available throughout the country.

In recent years there has been a photography explosion. Photographs have taken their place along with the traditional arts in galleries and museums across the nation, and photography books have been on best seller lists everywhere.

Artistic photography can be either documentary evidence depicting the world as it is through the photographer's eyes, or invention and fantasy showing the world as it can be imagined.

Pearl Jones, a San Francisco artist and photographer, welcomes the ever-increasing interest in photography as an art.

In 1969 Pearl went back to school to complete her undergraduate studies as a fine arts major at the University of California in Berkeley. There she learned how to develop prints and since then she's used photography as a tool in her art·work.

Photographer Pearl Jones

"Sometimes I start with a photograph and paint designs on it," she explains. "Or I use the self-timer to take pictures of myself engaged in different activities and dressed in various costumes."

A few of Pearl's prints are on exhibition at the San Francisco Art Institute where she heads part of the photography department. Others have appeared in galleries around town.

"Even though I've had several shows, I don't earn enough money to make a living as a photographer-artist. Very few people do. Most of us have part-time jobs teaching or processing film or working in another division of the field."

According to Pearl, it's difficult for newcomers to get any of the well-known galleries to show their works. She suggests that they contact those galleries which have open portfolio shows that are specifically geared to reveal new talents. *Art Week* magazine usually lists upcoming shows.

A cohesive, creative portfolio containing as few as five or as many as twenty-five pictures will help anyone anxious to get a career as an artist-photographer off the ground and onto the walls at exhibitions.

The staff at Hy Zazula Associates, Inc. in New York is made up of a different type of artist. What they do is on display day after day even though most of the public knows little about their work.

"Almost all of the ads viewed in newspapers, magazines and billboards have been retouched in one way or another," claims Steve Zazula.

Photoretouchers do anything and everything except actually take the pictures. They give beardless men beards, change the tint in a person's glasses—or remove the glasses altogether—clean up facial complexions and change blondes to redheads.

Most of their work is done for advertising agencies that feel something is missing or needed in a photograph that has been taken to promote a client or product.

"Agencies need photographers to take pictures and retouchers to perfect them," Steve says. His company, with thirty-five employees, is the largest of about forty retouching offices in New York.

In addition to changing pictures, Zazula Associates often combines pictures to form a single ad or photograph. For instance, a past cover of *Esquire* magazine showed Andy Warhol standing in a garbage can. Thanks to the artistic techniques of Zazula, people really thought Warhol posed in the garbage can when actually two separate photos were blended together to form one.

(Top) Unretouched photo
(Bottom) Same photo retouched by Hy Zazula Associates, Inc.

The company has even put together ads which combine as many as six different pictures.

According to Steve, "Retouchers don't have to be excellent photographers, but they should have a basic understanding of art, and knowing how to draw certainly helps."

More professional photographers—over 30,000—specialize in portrait and studio work than in any other area.

These are the people who take pictures of all kinds of celebrations, business meetings, families, babies, brides and grooms. Their job is to create personal mementos for customers, and the pictures they take often wind up in photo albums which are proudly displayed to friends and relatives.

While most studio photographers have their own studios staffed with camerapersons and lab technicians, it's not uncommon for the photographers to travel to peoples' homes and special events to take pictures.

Portrait photographer
Gerda Levy

Gerda Levy is the head photographer and manager of
Tonica Studios in San Francisco. She and the fifteen
camerapersons on staff specialize in children and family
portraits.

"I enjoy working with people and I love being able to
combine business skills and creative ability for my job,"
Gerda says.

A professional since 1944, Gerda has operated out of her
studio for nine years. She gets her customers through
referrals, personal contacts, promotions, and through an
exciting window display.

At Tonica Studios, the photographers take both posed and
candid shots.

"Wedding pictures are usually very traditional—the
bride gazing fondly at her ring, or the couple reflected in a
wine glass," Gerda explained.

"On the other hand, it's hard, if not impossible, to get a
child to hold still long enough to take a posed picture, so
those shots are very candid."

Gerda got her formal education in South America. While
she doesn't suggest future studio photographers travel that
far for schooling, she does recommend getting the proper
instruction.

"If you like the idea of operating your own studio, and
being directly responsible for your own success, then
portrait photography is the way to go," she said.

Randy Utell does very little picture taking. He prefers
working within a corporate structure as the assistant to the
product manager at Nikon, Inc.

He likes getting a bi-monthly paycheck and guaranteed
salary. He enjoys knowing most work days are from nine
until five.

That's not to imply Randy doesn't have a great love for
photography. His work revolves around cameras.

"Basically, mine is an administrative job," Randy ex-

plains. "I collect statistical data from the 2,500 to 3,000 authorized Nikon dealers and thirty repair shops in the United States. I deal with all the out-of-the-ordinary problems of consumers and dealers. I'm constantly interacting with other Nikon departments—educational services, repairs, orders, etc. I cover all bases."

According to Randy, he's usually holding the telephone in one hand taking a special order or listening to a unique complaint while he's writing a memo with his free hand.

"As much as I try to establish a routine, I know each day will bring the unexpected. When I get to work the phones are ringing endlessly and people are coming in with all sorts of emergency situations which demand immediate attention," he says.

For instance, a *National Geographic* editor recently phoned in because he needed to get hold of a particular Nikon camera for a special layout *National Geographic* was doing. Randy put him in touch with the proper dealer.

As assistant to the product manager, Randy finds his working knowledge of cameras and films essential to making it through the week. He serves as the prime source for all technical information within his division. He also compiles and maintains technical data for the manager.

Randy has held his specific job for two and a half years. Some employees work the same routine for twenty years while others move in and out of the various departments frequently.

"Working at Nikon is the ideal job for me and someone with similar interests because I'm able to use my love for photography to advance my career in the corporate world," Randy says.

Nikon representative Randy Utell

APPENDIX

Looking Toward a Future in Photography

In 1973–74 there were more than 83,700 students enrolled in motion picture, still photography and graphic art classes in the United States and Canada. At the same time there were 690 colleges and universities reporting one or more credit courses in these fields of instruction.

To help students (and parents) planning their futures, *A Survey of Motion Picture, Still Photography, and Graphic Arts Instruction* (T-17) was developed by Dr. C. William Horrell.

It, along with a list of the schools offering instruction, is available upon request from Dept. 454, Eastman Kodak Company, 343 State Street, Rochester, New York 14650.

A Directory of Colleges and Universities Offering Photography Instruction can be obtained from:
Education Committee
Professional Photographers of America, Inc.
1090 Executive Way
Des Plaines, Illinois 60018

Remember, whatever your interest, the opportunity is there, the variety is there, the excitement of working in a growing field is there, and, most importantly, the challenge is there.

INSTITUTIONS GRANTING SPECIFIC DEGREES WITH MAJOR EMPHASIS IN MOTION PICTURES, STILL PHOTOGRAPHY, AND/OR GRAPHIC ARTS

Certificates and Diplomas

California

ARTOGRAPHY ACADEMY OF PHOTO-GRAPHIC ARTS, 5352 Laurel Canyon Blvd., N. Hollywood 91607
Photography Dept.: Diploma in Still Photography

RIVERSIDE CITY COLLEGE, 4800 Magnolia St., Riverside 92506
Certificate in Graphic Arts and Still Photography

Florida

DAYTONA BEACH COMM. COLLEGE, Welch Blvd. at U.S. Route 92, P.O. Box 1111, Daytona Beach 32022
Photography Dept.: 2-Year Certificate in Still Photography

Maryland

VISUAL ARTS INSTITUTE, 1713 N. Charles St., Baltimore 21201
Graphic Arts and Photo Dept.: Certificate in Still Photography

Minnesota

ST. PAUL TECHNICAL-VOCATIONAL INSTITUTE, 235 Marshall St., St. Paul 55102
2-Year Diploma in Graphic Arts

Nebraska

KEARNEY STATE COLLEGE, 905 West 25th St., Kearney 68847
Industrial Ed Dept.: Endorsement in Graphic Arts

New York

NATIONAL TECHNICAL INSTITUTE FOR THE DEAF at R.I.T., Rochester 14623
Visual Communications Tech Dept.: Diploma for Printing Technology and Photographic Technician

Oklahoma

NORTHERN OKLAHOMA COLLEGE, 1220 E. Grand Ave., Tonkawa 74653
Journalism Dept.: 1-year Certificate in Graphic Arts

Texas

COLLEGE OF THE MAINLAND, 8001 Palmer Hwy., Texas City 77590
Learning Resources Dept.: 1-Year Diploma in Graphic Arts

Washington State

SEATTLE CENTRAL COMM. COLLEGE, 1718 Broadway, Seattle 98122
Photographic Dept.: Diploma in Still Photography

CONESTOGA COLLEGE OF APPLIED ARTS AND TECHNOLOGY, 299 Doon Valley Dr., Kitchener, Ontario
Communications and Design Dept.: 3-Year Diploma in Motion Pictures, Still Photography, and Graphic Arts
FANSHAWE COLLEGE, Oxford St. E., London, Ontario
Applied Arts Dept.: 2-Year Diploma, Photographic Technician; 3-Year Diploma in Photography
GEORGE BROWN COLLEGE OF APPLIED ARTS AND TECHNOLOGY, Box 1015, Sta. B., Toronto, Ontario M5T2T9

Graphic Arts Dept.: Diploma in Graphic Arts Printing or Graphic Design
RED RIVER COMM. COLLEGE, 2055 Notre Dame Ave., Winnipeg, Manitoba R3HOJ9
Creative Arts Dept.: Certificate of Attainment, Still Photography and Graphic Arts
VANCOUVER CITY COLLEGE, 100 W. 49th Ave., British Columbia V5Y2Z6
Cultural, Performing, and Applied Arts Dept.: 2-Year Diploma in Still Photography

AA or AS Degrees

Arizona

PHOENIX COLLEGE, 1202 W. Thomas Rd., Phoenix 85013
Photography Dept.: AA, Still Photography

California

BAKERSFIELD COLLEGE, 1801 Panorama Dr., Bakersfield 93305
Art Dept.: AA, Still Photography
CITRUS COLLEGE, 18824 E. Foothill Blvd., Azusa 91702
Industrial Tech, Public Service, Photo Dept.: AA, Still Photography
CITY COLLEGE OF SAN FRANCISCO, 50 Phelan Ave., San Francisco 94112
Printing Tech Dept.: AA, Graphic Arts
Photography and Cinematography Dept.: AA, Still Photography and Motion Pictures

COLLEGE OF SAN MATEO, 1700 W. Hillsdale Blvd., San Mateo 94402
Art Dept.: AA, Still Photography and Graphic Arts
CYPRESS COLLEGE, 9200 Valley View, Cypress 90630
Photography Dept.: AA, Still Photography
DE ANZA COLLEGE, 21250 Stevens Creek Blvd., Cupertino 95014
Photography Dept.: AA, Still Photography
EAST LOS ANGELES COLLEGE, 5357 Brooklyn Ave., Los Angeles 91801
Photography Dept.: AA, Still Photography
EL CAMINO COLLEGE, 16007 S. Crenshaw Blvd., Torrance 90506
Instruction Dept.: AA, Still Photography

FOOTHILL COLLEGE, 1234 El Monte Rd., Los Altos Hills 94022
Art Dept.: AA, Still Photography
FRESNO CITY COLLEGE, 1101 E. University Ave., Fresno 93741
Reprographic Dept.: AA and AS, Graphic Arts
GLENDALE COLLEGE, 1500 N. Verdugo Rd., Glendale 91208
Photography Dept.: AA, Still Photography
GOLDEN WEST COLLEGE, 15744 Golden West St., Huntington Beach 92647
Tech-Graphic Arts Dept.: AA, Graphic Arts
LANEY COLLEGE, 900 Fallon St., Oakland 94607
Photography Dept.: AS, Still Photography
LOS ANGELES VALLEY COLLEGE, 5800 Fulton Ave., Van Nuys 91401
Instruction Dept.: AA, Still Photography
Journalism Dept.: AA, Still Photography
Theatre and Cinema Arts Dept.: AA, Motion Pictures
MODESTO JR. COLLEGE, Modesto 95350
Art Dept.: AA, Graphic Arts
Trade and Technical Dept.: AA, Graphic Arts
MOORPARK COLLEGE, 7075 Campus Rd., Moorpark 93021
Photography Dept.: AA, Still Photography and Graphic Arts
MT. SAN ANTONIO COLLEGE, 1100 N. Grand Ave., Walnut 91789
Physical Science, Engineering, Graphics Dept.: AA, Still Photography
MT. SAN JACINTO COLLEGE, 21400 Hwy. 79, San Jacinto 92383
Photography Dept.: AS, Still Photography

Vocational Ed Dept.: AA, Still Photography and Graphic Arts
ORANGE COAST COLLEGE, 2701 Fairview Rd., Costa Mesa 92626
Photography Dept.: AA, Still Photography and Motion Pictures
Photography-Art Dept.: AA, Still Photography and Motion Pictures
PALOMAR COLLEGE, San Marcos 92069
Communications Dept.: AA, Still Photography
PASADENA CITY COLLEGE, 1570 E. Colorado Blvd., Pasadena 91106
Art Dept.: AA, Still Photography
Printing Dept.: AA, Graphic Arts
RIVERSIDE CITY COLLEGE, 4800 Magnolia, Riverside 92506
Photography Dept.: AA, Still Photography and Graphic Arts
SACRAMENTO CITY COLLEGE, 3835 Freeport Blvd., Sacramento 95822
Photography Dept.: AA, Graphic Arts
SKYLINE COLLEGE, 3300 College Dr., San Bruno 94066
Art Dept.: AA, Still Photography
SOLANO COMM. COLLEGE, P. O. Box 246, Suisun City 94585
Learning Resources Dept.: AS, Still Photography
VENTURA COLLEGE, 4667 Telegraph Rd., Ventura 93003
Photography Dept.: AA, Still Photography

Colorado

AIMS JR. COLLEGE, Box 69, Greeley 80631
Science-Math Dept.: AA, Graphic Arts
COLORADO MOUNTAIN COLLEGE, West Campus, Glenwood Springs 81601
Occupational Education Dept.: AAS, Still Photography
MESA COLLEGE, 1175 Texas Ave., Grand Junction 81501

Audio-Visual Dept.: AAS, Graphic Arts

Graphic Arts Dept.: AA, Graphic Arts

Connecticut

UNIVERSITY OF BRIDGEPORT, Bridgeport 06602

Art Dept.: AA, Still Photography

District of Columbia

WASHINGTON TECHNICAL INSTITUTE, 4100 Connecticut Ave., N.W., Washington 20008

Advertising Design Dept.: AA, Graphic Arts

Florida

BREVARD COMM. COLLEGE, Clear Lake Rd., Cocoa 32922

Industrial Photo Tech Dept.: AS, Still Photography

FLORIDA TECH UNIVERSITY, P.O. Box 25000, Orlando 32816

Art Dept.: AA, Still Photography, Motion Pictures, Graphic Arts

HILLSBOROUGH COMM. COLLEGE, P.O. Box 22127, Tampa 33622

Instructional Resources Dept.: AA, Graphic Arts

MIAMI-DADE COMM. COLLEGE, 11380 N.W. 27th Ave., Miami 33167

Graphic Arts Science, Commercial Art Dept.: AS, Graphic Arts

PALM BEACH JR. COLLEGE, 4200 S. Congress Ave., Lake Worth 33460

Art Dept.: AA, Still Photography and Graphic Arts; AS, Graphic Arts

PENSACOLA JR. COLLEGE, 1000 College Blvd., Pensacola 32504

Visual Arts Dept.: AA, Still Photography and Graphic Arts

POLK COMM. COLLEGE, 999 Avenue "H," N.E., Winter Haven 33880

Educational Media Dept.: AS, Media Technology

ST. PETERSBURG JR. COLLEGE, P.O. Box 13489, St. Petersburg 33733

Educational Planning and Research Dept.: AA, Motion Pictures

VALENCIA COMM. COLLEGE, 1800 S. Kirkman Rd., Valencia 32802

Technical and Engineering Dept.: AS, Graphic Arts

Georgia

MASSEY JR. COLLEGE, 56 Marietta St., Atlanta 30303

Photography Dept.: AA, Still Photography

Illinois

COLLEGE OF DUPAGE, Glen Ellyn 60137

Omega College: AA, Still Photography

Media Dept.: AA, Motion Picture

KENNEDY-KING COLLEGE, 6800 S. Wentworth Ave., Chicago 60621

Career Programs Dept.: AA, Graphic Arts

MCHENRY COUNTY COLLEGE, 6200 Northwest Highway, Crystal Lake 60014

Graphic Arts Dept.: AS, Graphic Arts

MORTON COLLEGE, Cicero 60650

Art Dept.: AA, Still Photography

TRITON COLLEGE, 2000 Fifth Ave., River Grove 60171

Education Dept.: AA, Still Photography and Graphic Arts

Indiana

BALL STATE UNIVERSITY, Muncie 47306

Industrial Ed and Tech Dept.: AA, Graphic Arts

VINCENNES UNIVERSITY, Vincennes 47591

Career Dept.: AS, Graphic Arts

Iowa

HAWKEYE INSTITUTE OF TECHNOLOGY, Box 8015, Waterloo 50704

Photography Dept.: AA, Still Photography

KIRKWOOD COMM. COLLEGE, 6301
Kirkwood Blvd., S.W., Cedar
Rapids 52406
Graphic Arts Dept.: AA, Graphic Arts

Kansas

HIGHLAND COMM. JR. COLLEGE, P.O.
Box 68, Highland 66035
AA, Graphic Arts

Kentucky

MOREHEAD STATE UNIVERSITY,
Morehead 40351
Industrial Ed Dept.: AA, Graphic Arts

Maine

CENTRAL MAINE VO-TECH INSTITUTE,
1250 Turner St., Auburn 04210
Graphic Arts Dept.: AA, Graphic Arts
ENDICOTT COLLEGE, Hale St., Bev-
erly 01915
Photography Dept.: AS, Still Photography

Maryland

CATONSVILLE COMM. COLLEGE, 800
S. Rolling Rd., Catonsville 21228
Art Dept.: AA, Graphic Arts
CECIL COMM. COLLEGE, North East
21901
Photography Dept.: AA, Still Photog-
raphy
MONTGOMERY COLLEGE, 51 Manakee
St., Rockville 20850
Visual Communications Tech Dept.:
AA, Still Photography and Graphic
Arts

Michigan

FERRIS STATE COLLEGE, Big Rapids
49307
Graphic Arts Dept.: AA, Still Photog-
raphy
HENRY FORD COMM. COLLEGE, 5101
Evergreen St., Dearborn 48128
Art Dept.: AA, Graphic Arts
MUSKEGON COMM. COLLEGE, 221 S.
Quarterline Rd., Muskegon 49442

Industrial Tech Dept.: AA, Graphic
Arts
WASHTENAW COMM. COLLEGE, Ann
Arbor 48106
Tech and Industrial Dept.: AA, Still
Photography

Minnesota

LAKEWOOD COMM. COLLEGE, White
Bear Lake 55110
Audio-Visual Dept.: AA, Graphic Arts
ROCHESTER COMM. COLLEGE,
Rochester 55901
Journalism Dept.: AA, Still Photogra-
phy

Missouri

CENTRAL MISSOURI STATE UNIVER-
SITY, Warrensburg 64093
Graphics Dept.: AA, Graphic Arts
FOREST PARK COMM. COLLEGE, 5600
Oakland Ave., St. Louis 63110
Art Dept.: AA, Graphic Arts
STEPHENS COLLEGE, Columbia 65201
Art Dept.: AA, Graphic Arts

Nebraska

CHADRON STATE COLLEGE, 10th and
Main Sts., Chadron 69337
Industrial Ed Dept.: AA, Graphic Arts

New Jersey

BROOKDALE COMM. COLLEGE, 765
Newman Springs Rd., Lincroft
07738
AAS, Graphic Design
MIDDLESEX COUNTY COLLEGE, Mill
Rd. and Woodbridge, Edison 08817
Art and Design Dept.: AS, Still Pho-
tography and Graphic Arts

New York

FASHION INSTITUTE OF TECH-
NOLOGY, West 27th St., New York
10001
Photography Dept.: AA, Still Photography

NASSAU COMM. COLLEGE, Stewart Ave., Garden City 11530
Communications Dept.: AA, Graphic Arts

NEW YORK COMM. COLLEGE, 300 Jay St., Brooklyn 11201
Graphic Arts and Advertising Technology Dept.: AAS, Graphic Arts

ROCHESTER INSTITUTE OF TECHNOLOGY, One Lomb Memorial Dr., Rochester 14623
Graphic Arts and Photography Dept.: AAS, Still Photography, Motion Pictures, and Graphic Arts

STATE UNIVERSITY, Farmingdale 11735
Photographic Technology Dept.: AA, Still Photography

North Carolina

CHOWAN COLLEGE, Murfreesboro 27855
Graphic Arts Dept.: AA, Still Photography, Graphic Arts

GUILFORD TECH INSTITUTE, P.O. Box 309, Jamestown 27282
Commercial Art and Photography Dept.: AA, Graphic Arts

RANDOLPH TECH INSTITUTE, P.O. Drawer 1009, Asheboro 27203
Photography Dept.: AA, Still Photography, Graphic Arts

TECH INSTITUTE OF ALAMANCE, 411 Camp Rd., Burlington 27215
AA, Graphic Arts

North Dakota

NORTH DAKOTA STATE SCHOOL OF SCIENCE, Wahpeton 58075
Special Services Dept.: AS, Graphic Arts

Ohio

CUYAHOGA COMM. COLLEGE, 7300 York Rd., Parma 44130
Graphic Communications Dept.: AA, Graphic Arts

LAKELAND COMM. COLLEGE, Mentor 44060
Business Tech Dept.: AAB, Applied Business

Oregon

LINN-BENTON COMM. COLLEGE, 6500 N.W. Pacific Blvd., Albany 97321
Humanities Dept.: AS, Graphic Communications

MT. HOOD COMM. COLLEGE, 26000 S.E. Stark St., Gresham 97030
Mass Communications Dept.: AA, Graphic Arts

PORTLAND COMM. COLLEGE, 12000 S.W. 49th Street, Portland 97219
Photo/Graphic Arts Dept.: AA, Graphic Arts

Pennsylvania

BUCKS COUNTY COMM. COLLEGE, Swamp Rd., Newtown 18940
Art Dept.: AA, Still Photography

COMM. COLLEGE OF PHILADELPHIA, 34 11th St., Philadelphia 19107
Photography Dept.: AA, Still Photography

THE WILLIAMSPORT AREA COMM. COLLEGE, 1005 W. Third St., Williamsport 17701
Graphic Arts Dept.: AS, Graphic Arts

South Dakota

BLACK HILLS STATE COLLEGE, 1200 University Ave., Black Hills 57783
Journalism Dept.: AA, Graphic Arts

NORTHERN STATE COLLEGE, 12th Ave. and Jay St., Aberdeen 57401
Industrial Arts and Safety Ed Dept.: AA, Graphic Arts

Texas

AMARILLO COLLEGE, 2200 Washington St., Amarillo 79178
Photographic Tech Dept.: AS, Still Photography

KILGORE JR. COLLEGE, 1100 Broadway Ave., Kilgore 75662

Technical–Vocational Dept.: AA, AS,
Graphic Arts
SAN ANTONIO COLLEGE, 1300 San
Pedro, San Antonio 78216
Physics, Engineering, Astronomy, and
Photography Dept.: AA, Motion
Pictures
SAN JACINTO COLLEGE, 8060 Spencer
Hwy., Pasadena 77505
Printing Technology Dept.: AA,
Graphic Arts
TEXAS STATE TECHNICAL INSTITUTE,
James Connally Campus, Waco
76705
Instructional Media Dept.: AS,
Graphic Arts

Utah
BRIGHAM YOUNG UNIVERSITY, Provo
84601
Communications and Art Dept.: AA,
Still Photography, Motion Pictures,
and Graphic Arts
UTAH TECH COLLEGE, PROVO, Box
1009, Provo 84601
Graphic Communications Dept.: AA,
Graphic Arts

Washington State
BELLEVUE COMM. COLLEGE, 3000
145th Place, S.E., Bellevue 98007
Art Dept.: AA, Graphic Arts
EVERETT COMM. COLLEGE, 801 Wet-
more Ave., Everett 98201
Photography Dept.: AA, Photography
SEATTLE CENTRAL COMM. COLLEGE,
1718 Broadway, Seattle 98122
Photography Dept.: AA, Still Photog-
raphy

West Virginia
FAIRMONT STATE COLLEGE, Locust
Ave., Fairmont 26554
Industrial Ed Dept.: AA

Wisconsin
MADISON AREA TECH COLLEGE, 221
N. Carroll St., Madison 53703
Art Dept.: AA, Still Photography and
Graphic Arts
MILWAUKEE AREA TECH COLLEGE,
1015 N. 6th Street, Milwaukee
53203
Printing and Publishing Dept.: AA,
Still Photography and Graphic Arts

BA or BS Degree

Alabama
UNIVERSITY OF ALABAMA, University
35486
Art Dept.: BA, Still Photography and
Graphic Arts

Arizona
ARIZONA STATE UNIVERSITY, Tempe
85281

Graphic Communications Dept.: BS,
BA, Graphic Arts

Arkansas
ARKANSAS STATE UNIVERSITY, P.O.
Box BBBB, State University 72467
Printing Dept.: BS, BSE, Graphic Arts

California

BROOKS INSTITUTE, 2190 Alston Rd., Santa Barbara 93108
BA, Still Photography

CALIFORNIA POLYTECHNIC STATE UNIVERSITY, San Luis Obispo 93407
Graphic Communications Dept.: BS, Graphic Arts

CALIFORNIA STATE UNIVERSITY, Chico 95926
Industry and Tech Dept.: BS, Graphic Arts

CALIFORNIA STATE UNIVERSITY, Fullerton 92634
Communications Dept.: BS, Still Photography and Motion Picture

CALIFORNIA STATE UNIVERSITY, Long Beach 90840
Industrial Ed Dept.: BA, Still Photography

CALIFORNIA STATE UNIVERSITY, Northridge 91324
Art Dept.: BA, Still Photography

CHAPMAN COLLEGE, 333 N. Glassell St., Orange 92666
Humanities Dept.: BA, Graphic Arts

DON BOSCO TECHNICAL INSTITUTE, 1151 San Gabriel Blvd., Rosemead 91770
Photolithography Tech Dept.: BS, Graphic Arts

FRESNO STATE UNIVERSITY, Cedar and Shaw, Fresno 93710
Industrial Arts and Tech Dept.: BS, Graphic Arts

SAN DIEGO STATE UNIVERSITY, 5402 College Ave., San Diego 92115
Telecommunications and Film Dept.: BS, BA, Motion Pictures
Industrial Arts Dept.: AB, Graphic Arts

UNIVERSITY OF CALIFORNIA, Davis 95616
Art Dept.: AB, Still Photography, Motion Pictures, and Graphic Arts

UNIVERSITY OF CALIFORNIA, LOS ANGELES, 405 Hilgard Ave., Los Angeles 90024
Theatre Arts Dept.: BS, Motion Pictures

UNIVERSITY OF THE PACIFIC, 3601 Pacific Ave., Stockton 95204
Art Dept.: BA, Graphic Arts

UNIVERSITY OF SOUTHERN CALIFORNIA, University Park, Los Angeles 90007
Cinema Dept.: BA, Motion Pictures

Colorado

UNIVERSITY OF COLORADO, Boulder 80302
Art Dept.: BA, Still Photography

UNIVERSITY OF NORTHERN COLORADO, Greeley 80631
Industrial Arts Dept.: BS, Graphic Arts

Connecticut

CENTRAL CONNECTICUT STATE COLLEGE, 1615 Stanley St., New Britain 06050
Research Dept.: BS, Graphic Arts

UNIVERSITY OF BRIDGEPORT, Bridgeport 06602
Art Dept.: BS, Graphic Arts; BA, Motion Pictures

District of Columbia

HOWARD UNIVERSITY SCHOOL OF COMMUNICATIONS, 2400 6th St. N.W., Washington 20001
BA, Motion Pictures

Florida

FLORIDA ATLANTIC UNIVERSITY, Boca Raton 33432
Art Dept.: BA, Still Photography

FLORIDA TECH UNIVERSITY, P.O. Box 25000, Orlando 32816
Art Dept.: BA, Still Photography, Motion Pictures and Graphic Arts

UNIVERSITY OF NORTH FLORIDA, Jacksonville 32216
Art Dept.: BA, Graphic Arts

Georgia

BRENAU COLLEGE, Gainsville 30501
BA, Graphic Arts
GEORGIA SOUTHWESTERN COLLEGE, Americus 31709
Art Dept.: BS, Still Photography and Graphic Arts
UNIVERSITY OF GEORGIA, Athens 30602
Art Dept.: AB, Motion Pictures

Hawaii

UNIVERSITY OF HAWAII, HILO, Hilo 96720
Art Dept.: BA, Graphic Arts

Illinois

BRADLEY UNIVERSITY, Peoria 61606
Art Dept.: BS, Still Photography, Motion Pictures, and Graphic Arts
EASTERN ILLINOIS UNIVERSITY, Charleston 61920
Industrial Ed. Dept.: BS, Graphic Arts
ILLINOIS INSTITUTE OF TECHNOLOGY, 3300 Federal St., Chicago 60616
Photography Dept.: BS, Still Photography and Motion Pictures
ILLINOIS STATE UNIVERSITY, Normal 61761
Industrial Tech Dept.: BS, Graphic Arts
NORTHERN ILLINOIS UNIVERSITY, DeKalb 60115
Industry and Tech—Graphic Arts Dept.: BS, Graphic Arts
NORTHWESTERN UNIVERSITY, Evanston 60201
Radio—TV—Film Dept.: BS, Motion Pictures
SOUTHERN ILLINOIS UNIVERSITY, Carbondale 62901
Cinema and Photography Dept.: BS, Still Photography and Motion Pictures

Indiana

BALL STATE UNIVERSITY, Muncie 47306
Art Dept.: BS, Graphic Arts
Journalism Dept.: BA, Still Photography
Industrial Ed and Tech Dept.: BS, Graphic Arts
INDIANA STATE UNIVERSITY, Terre Haute 47809
Art Dept.: BS, Still Photography
PURDUE UNIVERSITY, W. Lafayette 47007
English Dept.: BA, Motion Pictures
UNIVERSITY OF NOTRE DAME, Notre Dame 46556
Art Dept.: BA, Still Photography

Iowa

DRAKE UNIVERSITY, 25th and University Aves., Des Moines 50311
Journalism Dept.: BA, Graphic Arts

Kansas

HAYS KANSAS STATE COLLEGE, Hays 67601
Dept.: BA, Graphic Arts
KANSAS STATE COLLEGE, PITTSBURG, Pittsburg 66762
Instructional Media Dept.: BS, Graphic Arts
Printing Dept.: BS, Graphic Arts
UNIVERSITY OF KANSAS, Flint Hall, Lawrence 66045
Journalism Dept.: BS, Still Photography and Motion Pictures
UNIVERSITY OF KANSAS, Lawrence 66045
Radio—TV—Film Dept.: BS, Still Photography

Kentucky

MOREHEAD STATE UNIVERSITY, Morehead 40351
Industrial Ed Dept.: BS, Graphic Arts
UNIVERSITY OF LOUISVILLE, Louisville 40208
Art Dept.: BS, Still Photography

WESTERN KENTUCKY UNIVERSITY, Bowling Green 42101

Mass Communications and Educational TV Dept.: BS, Still Photography and Motion Pictures

Louisiana

LOUISIANA STATE UNIVERSITY, New Orleans 70122

Drama and Communications Dept.: BA, Motion Pictures

Maine

UNIVERSITY OF MAINE, PORTLAND—GORHAM, Gorham 04038

Graphic Arts Dept.: BS, Graphic Arts

Maryland

LOYOLA COLLEGE, 4501 N. Charles St., Baltimore 21210

Communications Arts Dept.: BA, Still Photography

Michigan

CENTRAL MICHIGAN UNIVERSITY, Mt. Pleasant 48859

Art Dept.: BS, Graphic Arts

FERRIS STATE COLLEGE, Big Rapids 49307

Graphic Arts Dept.: BS, Graphic Arts

GRAND VALLEY STATE COLLEGE, Allendale 49401

BS, Graphic Arts

HOPE COLLEGE, Holland 49423

AB, Graphic Arts

NORTHERN MICHIGAN UNIVERSITY, Marquette 49855

BS, Graphic Arts

WESTERN MICHIGAN UNIVERSITY, Kalamazoo 49001

Industrial Ed Dept.: BS, Graphic Arts
Art Dept.: BS, Still Photography

Minnesota

BEMIDJI STATE COLLEGE, Bemidji 55601

Communications Dept.: BS, Still Photography and Graphic Arts
Industrial Ed Dept.: BS, Graphic Arts

ST. CATHERINE'S COLLEGE, St. Paul 55105

Theatre Arts Dept.: BA, Graphic Arts

ST. MARY'S COLLEGE, Winona 55987

Communications Dept.: BA, Graphic Arts

UNIVERSITY OF MINNESOTA, West Bank, Minneapolis 55455

Studio Arts Dept.: BA, Still Photography

Missouri

CENTRAL MISSOURI STATE UNIVERSITY, Warrensburg 64093

Graphic Dept.: BS, Graphic Arts

STEPHENS COLLEGE, Columbia 65201

Art Dept.: BA, Graphic Arts

UNIVERSITY OF MISSOURI, 100 Neff Hall, Columbia 65201

Journalism Dept.: BA, Still Photography

WEBSTER COLLEGE, 470 E. Lockwood, Webster Groves 63119

Art Dept.: BA, Still Photography and Motion Pictures

Montana

MONTANA STATE UNIVERSITY, Bozeman 59715

Film and Television Dept.: BS, Still Photography

Nebraska

CONCORDIA COLLEGE, 800 Columbia Ave., Seward 68434

Humanities Dept.: BS, Graphic Arts; BS, Ed.; and BA, Graphic Arts

CREIGHTON UNIVERSITY, 2500 California St., Omaha 68178

Art Dept.: BA, Still Photography and Motion Pictures

New Jersey

KEAN COLLEGE OF NEW JERSEY, Morris Ave., Union 07083

Industrial Studies Dept.: BS, Graphic Arts

MONTCLAIR STATE COLLEGE, Valley Rd. and Normal Ave., Montclair 07043
Industrial Ed and Tech Dept.: BS, Graphic Arts
MONTCLAIR STATE COLLEGE, Upper Montclair 07043
Art Dept.: BA, Still Photography, Motion Pictures, and Graphic Arts
SETON HALL UNIVERSITY, S. Orange Ave., South Orange 07079
Communications Dept.: BA, Motion Pictures
TRENTON STATE COLLEGE, Trenton 08625
Industrial Ed Dept.: BA, Graphic Arts

New Mexico
NEW MEXICO STATE UNIVERSITY, University Park, Las Cruces 88003
Journalism and Mass Communications Dept.: BA, Still Photography, Motion Pictures

New York
ITHACA COLLEGE, Ithaca 14850
Communications Dept.: BS, Still Photography and Motion Pictures
NAZARETH COLLEGE OF ROCHESTER, 4245 East Ave., Rochester 14610
Photography Dept.: BA, Still Photography
RICHMOND COLLEGE, City University of New York, Staten Island 10301
Humanities Dept.: BA, Motion Pictures
ROCHESTER INSTITUTE OF TECHNOLOGY, One Lomb Memorial Dr., Rochester 14623
Graphic Arts and Photo Dept.: BS, Still Photography, Motion Pictures, and Graphic Arts
STATE UNIVERSITY OF NEW YORK, BINGHAMTON, Vestal Parkway E., Binghamton 13901
Cinema Dept.: BA, Motion Pictures

SYRACUSE UNIVERSITY, Syracuse 13210
Photography Dept.: BA, BS, Still Photography, Motion Pictures, and Graphic Arts

North Carolina
APPALACHIAN STATE UNIVERSITY, Boone 28607
Industrial Arts and Technical Education Dept.: BS, Graphic Arts
UNIVERSITY OF NORTH CAROLINA, Swain Hall, Chapel Hill 27514
Radio, TV, and Motion Picture Dept.: BA, Motion Pictures

Ohio
BOWLING GREEN STATE UNIVERSITY, Bowling Green 43403
Industrial Ed and Tech Dept.: BS, Still Photography, Motion Pictures and Graphic Arts
MIAMI UNIVERSITY, Oxford 45056
Industrial Ed Dept.: BS, Graphic Arts
MIAMI UNIVERSITY, MIDDLETOWN BRANCH, Middletown 45056
Industrial Ed—Photography Dept.: BS, Graphic Arts
THE OHIO STATE UNIVERSITY, 156 W. 19th Ave., Columbus 43210
Photography and Cinema Dept.: BS, Still Photography and Motion Pictures
UNIVERSITY OF TOLEDO, 2801 W. Bancroft St., Toledo 43606
Theatre Dept.: BA, Motion Pictures
WRIGHT STATE UNIVERSITY, Dayton 45431
Theatre Dept.: BA, Motion Pictures

Pennsylvania
CHENEY STATE COLLEGE, Cheney 19319
Industrial Art Dept.: BS, Graphic Arts
TEMPLE UNIVERSITY, Philadelphia 19122
Radio—TV—Film Dept.: BA, Motion Pictures

Rhode Island

ROGER WILLIAMS COLLEGE, Ferry Rd., Bristol 02809
Film Area Studies Dept.: BA, Motion Pictures

South Carolina

BOB JONES UNIVERSITY, Greenville 29614
Unusual Film Dept.: BS, Motion Pictures

Tennessee

EAST TENNESSEE STATE UNIVERSITY, Johnson City 37601
Art Dept.: BS, Graphic Arts
MEMPHIS STATE UNIVERSITY, Memphis 38152
Radio—TV—Film Dept.: BA, Motion Pictures

Texas

EAST TEXAS STATE UNIVERSITY, Commerce 75428
Audio-Visual Dept.: BS, Graphic Arts, Still Photography
Journalism and Graphic Arts Dept.: BS, Still Photography and Graphic Arts
SAM HOUSTON STATE UNIVERSITY, Huntsville 77340
Industrial Ed and Tech Dept.: BA, Still Photography, BS, Graphic Arts
STEPHEN F. AUSTIN STATE UNIVERSITY, Box 6073 SFA, Nacogdoches 75961
Communications Dept.: BS, BA, Still Photography
SUL ROSS STATE UNIVERSITY, P.O. Box 6065, Alpine 79830
Industrial Arts Dept.: BS, Graphic Arts
TEXAS A. & I. UNIVERSITY, 6300 Ocean Dr., Corpus Christi 78411
Education and Media Dept.: BS, Graphic Arts
TRINITY UNIVERSITY, 715 Stadium Dr., San Antonio 78284

Journalism, Broadcasting, and Film Dept.: BA, Motion Pictures
UNIVERSITY OF TEXAS, AUSTIN, Austin 78712
Radio, TV, Film Dept.: BS, Motion Pictures

Utah

BRIGHAM YOUNG UNIVERSITY, Provo 84601
Communications and Art Dept.: BS, Motion Pictures, Still Photography, and Graphic Arts
UNIVERSITY OF UTAH, Salt Lake City 84112
Communications Dept.: BS, Still Photography and Motion Pictures
UTAH STATE UNIVERSITY, Logan 84322
Art Dept.: BA, Still Photography

Vermont

GODDARD COLLEGE, Plainfield 05667
BA, Motion Pictures, Still Photography

Washington State

CENTRAL WASHINGTON STATE COLLEGE, Ellensburg 98926
Art Dept.: BA, Still Photography

West Virginia

FAIRMONT STATE COLLEGE, Locust Ave., Fairmont 26554
Industrial Education Dept.: BS, Graphic Arts

Wisconsin

UNIVERSITY OF WISCONSIN, Madison 53706
Art Dept.: BS, Still Photography, Graphic Arts
UNIVERSITY OF WISCONSIN, 821 University Ave., Madison 53706
Communications Dept.: BA, Motion Pictures
UNIVERSITY OF WISCONSIN, STOUT, Menomonie 54751
Graphic Communications Dept.: BS, Graphic Arts

CANADA

FANSHAWE COLLEGE, Oxford St. E., London, Ontario
Design Dept.: BS, Graphic Arts
RYERSON POLYTECHNICAL INSTITUTE, 50 Gould St., Toronto, Ontario M5B1E8
Photographic Arts Dept.: BA, Still Photography and Motion Pictures
SIR GEORGE WILLIAMS UNIVERSITY, Montreal, Quebec 109

Art Dept.: BA, Motion Pictures
UNIVERSITY OF QUEBEC, MONTREAL, 125 Ouest Sherbrooke, Montreal
Art Dept.: BS, Graphic Arts
UNIVERSITY OF WINDSOR, Windsor, Ontario N9B3P4
Communications Dept.: BA, Motion Pictures
YORK UNIVERSITY, 4700 Keele St., Downsview, Toronto, Ontario
Film Dept.: BA, Still Photography and Graphic Arts

BFA or Other
Bachelor's Degrees

Alabama

UNIVERSITY OF ALABAMA, University 35486
Art Dept.: BFA, Still Photography and Graphic Arts

Arizona

ARIZONA STATE UNIVERSITY, Tempe 85281
Art Dept.: BFA, Still Photography and Graphic Arts

California

CALIFORNIA COLLEGE OF ARTS AND CRAFTS, 5212 Broadway, Oakland 94618
Art Dept.: BFA, Still Photography
Media Dept.: BFA, Still Photography and Graphic Arts
SAN FRANCISCO ART INSTITUTE, 800 Chestnut St., 94133
Filmmaking Dept.: BFA, Motion Pictures
Photo Dept.: BFA, Still Photography

Colorado

UNIVERSITY OF COLORADO, Boulder 80302
Art Dept.: BFA, Still Photography

Connecticut

UNIVERSITY OF BRIDGEPORT, Bridgeport 06602
Theatre and Cinema Dept.: BFA, Motion Pictures
UNIVERSITY OF HARTFORD, 200 Bloomfield Ave., West Hartford 06117
Photography Dept.: BFA, Still Photography, Motion Pictures

Florida

BARRY COLLEGE, 11300 N.E. Second Ave., Miami 33161
Art Dept.: BFA, Still Photography and Graphic Arts
FLORIDA STATE UNIVERSITY, Tallahassee 32306
Art Dept.: BFA, Still Photography and Motion Pictures

FLORIDA TECH UNIVERSITY, P.O. Box 25000, Orlando 32816
Art Dept.: BFA, Still Photography, Motion Pictures, Graphic Arts
PENSACOLA JR. COLLEGE, 1000 College Blvd., Pensacola 32504
Visual Arts Dept.: BFA, Still Photography and Graphic Arts

Georgia

GEORGIA STATE UNIVERSITY, 33 Gilmer St., Atlanta 30303
Art Dept.: BFA, Still Photography and Graphic Arts
UNIVERSITY OF GEORGIA, Athens 30602
Art Dept.: BFA, Still Photography

Illinois

THE ART INSTITUTE OF CHICAGO, Michigan at Adams, Chicago 60603
Photography Dept.: BFA, Still Photography
BRADLEY UNIVERSITY, Peoria 61606
Art Dept.: BFA, Still Photography, Motion Pictures, and Graphic Arts
UNIVERSITY OF ILLINOIS, URBANA, 143 Fine Arts Bldg., Urbana 61820
Art and Design Dept.: BFA, Graphic Arts

Indiana

UNIVERSITY OF NOTRE DAME, Notre Dame 46556
Art Dept.: BFA, Still Photography

Iowa

UNIVERSITY OF IOWA, 204 Communications Ctr., Iowa City 52242
Journalism Dept.: BFA, Still Photography
Art Dept.: BFA, Still Photography and Graphic Arts

Kansas

WICHITA STATE UNIVERSITY, 1845 Fairmount, Wichita 67208
Graphic Design Dept.: BFA, Graphic Arts

Kentucky

WESTERN KENTUCKY UNIVERSITY, Bowling Green 42101
Mass Communications and Educational TV Dept.: BFA, Still Photography and Motion Pictures

Louisiana

LOUISIANA TECH UNIVERSITY, Ruston 71270
Art Dept.: BFA, Still Photography

Maryland

MARYLAND INSTITUTE COLLEGE OF ART, 1300 Mount Royal Ave., Baltimore 21217
Photography Dept.: BFA, Still Photography

Michigan

THE ART SCHOOL OF THE SOCIETY OF ARTS AND CRAFTS, 245 E. Kirby, Detroit 48202
Photography Dept.: BFA, Still Photography
CENTRAL MICHIGAN UNIVERSITY, Mt. Pleasant 48859
Art Dept.: BFA, Still Photography
EASTERN MICHIGAN UNIVERSITY, Ypsilanti 48197
Art Dept.: BFA, Still Photography
UNIVERSITY OF MICHIGAN, Ann Arbor 48104
Art Dept.: BFA, Still Photography

Minnesota

MINNEAPOLIS COLLEGE OF ART AND DESIGN, 55404
Design Dept.: BFA, Still Photography and Graphic Arts

Mississippi

JACKSON STATE COLLEGE, Jackson 39217
Art Dept.: BFA, Graphic Arts

Missouri

KANSAS CITY ART INSTITUTE, 4415 Warwick Blvd., Kansas City 64111

Photography and Cinema Dept.: BFA, Still Photography

NORTHWEST MISSOURI STATE UNIVERSITY, Maryville 64468
Art Dept.: BFA, Still Photography

STEPHENS COLLEGE, Columbia 65201
Art Dept.: BFA, Graphic Arts

Nebraska

CREIGHTON UNIVERSITY, 2500 California St., Omaha 68178
Art Dept.: BFA, Still Photography

UNIVERSITY OF NEBRASKA, Lincoln 68508
Art Dept.: BFA, Still Photography and Graphic Arts

New Mexico

THE UNIVERSITY OF NEW MEXICO, Albuquerque 87131
Art Dept.: BFA, Still Photography

New York

THE COOPER UNION ART SCHOOL, Cooper Square, New York 10003
Photography Dept.: BFA, Graphic Arts

NEW YORK UNIVERSITY, Washington Square, New York 10003
Film—TV Dept.: BFA, Motion Pictures

NEW YORK INSTITUTE OF TECHNOLOGY, Old Westbury, Long Island 11568
Art Dept.: BFA, Motion Pictures

C. W. POST COLLEGE, LONG ISLAND UNIVERSITY, Greenvale 11548
Theatre Arts Dept.: BFA, Motion Pictures

PRATT INSTITUTE, Brooklyn 11205
Film Dept.: BFA, Motion Pictures
Photography Dept.: BFA, Still Photography

ROCHESTER INSTITUTE OF TECHNOLOGY, One Lomb Memorial Dr., Rochester 14623
Graphic Arts and Photography Dept.:

BFA, Still Photography, Motion Pictures, and Graphic Arts

SCHOOL OF VISUAL ARTS, 209 E. 23rd St., New York 10010
Photography Dept.: BFA, Still Photography

Ohio

COLLEGE OF THE DAYTON ART INSTITUTE, 456 Belmont Park N., Dayton 45405
Photography and Design Dept.: BFA, Still Photography

OHIO UNIVERSITY, Athens 45701
Photography Dept.: BFA, Still Photography

WRIGHT STATE UNIVERSITY, Dayton 45431
Art Dept.: BFA, Still Photography and Motion Pictures

Pennsylvania

PHILADELPHIA COLLEGE OF ART, Broad and Pine Sts., Philadelphia 19102
Photography—Film Dept.: BFA, Still Photography and Motion Pictures

Rhode Island

UNIVERSITY OF RHODE ISLAND, Kingston 02881
Art Dept.: BFA, Still Photography

Tennessee

EAST TENNESSEE STATE UNIVERSITY, Johnson City 37601
Art Dept.: BFA, Still Photography

MEMPHIS ACADEMY OF ARTS, Overton Park 38112
Photography Dept.: BFA, Still Photography

Texas

NORTH TEXAS STATE UNIVERSITY, Denton 76203
Art Dept.: BFA, Still Photography

SOUTHERN METHODIST UNIVERSITY, Dallas 75275

Broadcast—Film Arts Dept.: BFA, Motion Pictures and Graphic Arts

STEPHEN F. AUSTIN UNIVERSITY, Box 6073, SFA, Nacogdoches 75961
Communication Dept.: BFA, Still Photography

Utah

BRIGHAM YOUNG UNIVERSITY, Provo 84601
Communications and Art Dept.: BFA, Still Photography, Motion Pictures, and Graphic Arts

UTAH STATE UNIVERSITY, Logan 84322
Art Dept.: BFA, Still Photography

Vermont

WINDHAM COLLEGE, Putney 05346
Art Dept.: BFA, Still Photography

CANADA

UNIVERSITY OF ALBERTA, Edmonton, Alberta T6G0X7
Art and Design Dept.: BFA, Still Photography

MA or MS Degree

Alabama

UNIVERSITY OF ALABAMA, University 35486
Art Dept.: MS, MA, Still Photography

Arizona

ARIZONA STATE UNIVERSITY, Tempe 85281
Graphic Communications Dept.: MS, MA, Graphic Arts

California

CALIFORNIA STATE UNIVERSITY, Fullerton 92634
Communications Dept.: MS, MA, Still Photography and Motion Pictures

CALIFORNIA STATE UNIVERSITY, LOS ANGELES, Los Angeles 90032
Industrial Studies Dept.: MS, MA, Still Photography

CALIFORNIA STATE UNIVERSITY, FRESNO, Fresno 93710
Journalism Dept.: MA, Still Photography

SAN DIEGO STATE UNIVERSITY, 5402 College Ave., San Diego 92115
Telecommunications and Film Dept.: MS, MA, Motion Pictures

SCHOOL OF THEOLOGY, 1325 N. College, Claremont 91711
Communication Arts Dept.: MS, MA, Motion Pictures

STANFORD UNIVERSITY, Stanford 94305
Communications Dept.: MA, MS, Motion Pictures

UNIVERSITY OF SOUTHERN CALIFORNIA, University Park, Los Angeles 90007
Cinema Dept.: MA, Motion Pictures; MS, Film Editing

Colorado

UNIVERSITY OF NORTHERN COLORADO, Greeley 80631
Industrial Arts Dept.: MA, Graphic Arts

Connecticut

CENTRAL CONNECTICUT STATE COLLEGE, 1615 Stanley St., New Britain 06050
Research Dept.: MA, MS, Graphic Arts
UNIVERSITY OF CONNECTICUT, Box U—127, Storrs 06268
Dramatic Arts Dept.: MS, MA, Motion Pictures

District of Columbia

THE AMERICAN UNIVERSITY, Washington 20016
Communications Dept.: MA, Motion Pictures and Still Photography

Georgia

UNIVERSITY OF GEORGIA, Athens 30602
Journalism Dept.: MA, Motion Pictures

Illinois

ILLINOIS INSTITUTE OF TECHNOLOGY, 3300 Federal St., Chicago 60616
Photography Dept.: MS, MA, Still Photography and Motion Pictures
ILLINOIS STATE UNIVERSITY, Normal 61761
Art Dept.: MS, MA, Still Photography
Industrial Tech Dept.: MS, MA, Graphic Arts
NORTHERN ILLINOIS UNIVERSITY, DeKalb 60115
Art Dept.: MA, MS, Still Photography
Industry, Technology, and Graphic Arts Dept.: MA, MS, Graphic Arts
NORTHWESTERN UNIVERSITY, Evanston 60201
Radio, TV, and Film Dept.: MA, MS, Motion Pictures
SOUTHERN ILLINOIS UNIVERSITY, Carbondale 62901
Cinema and Photography Dept.: MS, MA, Still Photography and Motion Pictures

Indiana

BALL STATE UNIVERSITY, Muncie 47306
Journalism Dept.: MA, MS, Still Photography
PURDUE UNIVERSITY, W. Lafayette 47907
Art Dept.: MA, MS, Still Photography
NOTRE DAME UNIVERSITY, Notre Dame 46556
Art Dept.: MA, MS, Still Photography

Iowa

UNIVERSITY OF IOWA, Iowa City 52240
Art Dept.: MA, MS, Still Photography and Graphic Arts
UNIVERSITY OF NORTHERN IOWA, Cedar Falls 50613
Industrial Arts and Technology Dept.: MA, MS, Graphic Arts

Kansas

KANSAS STATE COLLEGE, PITTSBURG, Pittsburg 66762
Printing Dept.: MS, MA, Graphic Arts
UNIVERSITY OF KANSAS, Lawrence 66045
Journalism Dept.: MS, MA, Motion Pictures

Louisiana

LOUISIANA STATE UNIVERSITY, New Orleans 70122
Drama and Communications Dept.: MA, MS, Motion Pictures

Maine

UNIVERSITY OF MAINE, PORTLAND— GORHAM, Gorham 04038
Graphic Arts Dept.: MA, MS, Graphic Arts

Michigan

CENTRAL MICHIGAN UNIVERSITY, Mt. Pleasant 48859
Art Dept.: MA, Still Photography
UNIVERSITY OF MICHIGAN, Ann Arbor 48104

Art Dept.: MS, MA, Still Photography
WESTERN MICHIGAN UNIVERSITY, Kalamazoo 49001
Art Dept.: MS, MA, Still Photography

Minnesota
BEMIDJI STATE COLLEGE, Bemidji 55601
Communications Dept.: MS, MA, Graphic Arts

Missouri
CENTRAL MISSOURI STATE UNIVERSITY, Warrensburg 64093
MS, MA, Graphic Arts
UNIVERSITY OF MISSOURI, 100 Neff Hall, Columbia 65201
Journalism Dept.: MA, Still Photography
WEBSTER COLLEGE, 470 E. Lockwood, St. Louis 63119
Art Dept.: MAT, Still Photography and Graphic Arts

New Jersey
MONTCLAIR STATE COLLEGE, Upper Montclair 07043
Industrial Education and Technology Dept.: MA, Still Photography, Motion Pictures, and Graphic Arts

New Mexico
THE UNIVERSITY OF NEW MEXICO, Albuquerque 87131
Art Dept.: MS, MA, Still Photography

New York
ITHACA COLLEGE, Ithaca 14850
Communications Dept.: MA, MS, Communications
NEW YORK UNIVERSITY, 80 Washington Sq. East, New York 10003
Art Ed Dept.: MS, MA, Still Photography

C. W. POST COLLEGE OF LONG ISLAND UNIVERSITY, Greenvale 11548
Art Dept.: MA, MS, Still Photography
ROCHESTER INSTITUTE OF TECHNOLOGY, One Lomb Memorial Dr., Rochester 14623
Graphic Arts and Photography Dept.: MS, Still Photography, Motion Pictures, and Graphic Arts
STATE UNIVERSITY OF NEW YORK, BUFFALO, Butler Annex A-8, Buffalo 14214
Media Study Dept.: MA, Motion Pictures

Ohio
OHIO UNIVERSITY, Athens 45701
Photography Dept.: MS, MA, Still Photography

South Carolina
BOB JONES UNIVERSITY, Greenville 29614
Unusual Film Dept.: MS, MA, Motion Pictures

Washington State
CENTRAL WASHINGTON STATE COLLEGE, Ellensburg 98926
Art Dept.: MA, MS, Still Photography

Wisconsin
UNIVERSITY OF WISCONSIN, Madison 53706
Art Dept.: MS, MA, Still Photography and Graphic Arts
UNIVERSITY OF WISCONSIN, 821 University Ave., Madison 53706
Communications Dept.: MA, MS, Motion Pictures
UNIVERSITY OF WISCONSIN, STOUT, Menomonie 54751
Graphic Communications Dept.: MA, MS, Graphic Arts

MFA or Other Master's Degrees

Alabama

UNIVERSITY OF ALABAMA, University 35486
Art Dept.: MFA, Still Photography

Arizona

ARIZONA STATE UNIVERSITY, Tempe 85281
Art Dept.: MFA, Still Photography and Graphic Arts

California

CALIFORNIA COLLEGE OF ARTS AND CRAFTS, 5212 Broadway, Oakland 94618
Film Dept.: MFA, Still Photography and Motion Pictures
Media Dept.: MFA, Still Photography and Graphic Arts
SAN FRANCISCO ART INSTITUTE, 800 Chestnut St., San Francisco 94133
Filmmaking Dept.: MFA, Motion Pictures
Photography Dept.: MFA, Still Photography
UNIVERSITY OF CALIFORNIA, Davis 95616
Art Dept.: MFA, Still Photography, Motion Pictures, and Graphic Arts
UNIVERSITY OF CALIFORNIA, LOS ANGELES, 405 Hilgard Ave., Los Angeles 90024
Theatre Arts Dept.: MFA, Motion Pictures
UNIVERSITY OF SOUTHERN CALIFORNIA, University Park, Los Angeles 90007
Cinema Dept.: MFA, Motion Pictures

Colorado

UNIVERSITY OF COLORADO, Boulder 80302
Art Dept.: MFA, Still Photography

Connecticut

UNIVERSITY OF HARTFORD, 200 Bloomfield Ave., West Hartford 06117
Photography Dept.: MFA, Still Photography and Motion Pictures

Florida

UNIVERSITY OF SOUTH FLORIDA, Fowler Ave., Tampa 33620
Art Dept.: MFA, Still Photography and Motion Pictures

Georgia

GEORGIA STATE UNIVERSITY, 33 Gilmer St., Atlanta 30303
Art Dept.: MFA, Still Photography and Graphic Arts
UNIVERSITY OF GEORGIA, Athens 30602
Art Dept.: MFA, Still Photography

Illinois

THE ART INSTITUTE OF CHICAGO, Michigan at Adams, Chicago 60603
Photography Dept.: MFA, Still Photography
BRADLEY UNIVERSITY, Peoria 61606
Art Dept.: MFA, Still Photography, Motion Pictures, and Graphic Arts
NORTHERN ILLINOIS UNIVERSITY, DeKalb 60115
Art Dept.: MFA, Still Photography
NORTHWESTERN UNIVERSITY, Evanston 60201
Radio—TV—Film Dept.: MFA, Motion Pictures
UNIVERSITY OF ILLINOIS, URBANA, 143 Fine Arts Bldg., Urbana 61821
Art and Design Dept.: MFA, Still Photography, Motion Pictures and Graphic Arts

Indiana

NOTRE DAME UNIVERSITY, Notre Dame 46556
Art Dept.: MFA, Still Photography

Iowa

UNIVERSITY OF IOWA, 204 Communications Ctr., Iowa City 52242
Journalism Dept.: MFA, Still Photography
Art Dept.: MFA, Still Photography and Graphic Arts

Louisiana

LOUISIANA STATE UNIVERSITY, New Orleans 70122
Drama and Communications Dept.: MFA, Motion Pictures
LOUISIANA TECH UNIVERSITY, Ruston 71270
Art Dept.: MFA, Still Photography

Maryland

MARYLAND INSTITUTE COLLEGE OF ART, 1300 Mount Royal Ave., Baltimore 21217
Photography Dept.: MFA, Still Photography

Michigan

EASTERN MICHIGAN UNIVERSITY, Ypsilanti 48197
Art Dept.: MFA, Still Photography
UNIVERSITY OF MICHIGAN, Ann Arbor 48104
Art Dept.: MFA, Still Photography
WESTERN MICHIGAN UNIVERSITY, Kalamazoo 49001
Art Dept.: MFA, Still Photography

Minnesota

UNIVERSITY OF MINNESOTA, West Bank, Minneapolis 55455
Art Dept.: MFA, Still Photography

Nebraska

UNIVERSITY OF NEBRASKA, Lincoln 68508
Art Dept.: MFA, Still Photography

New Mexico

THE UNIVERSITY OF NEW MEXICO, Albuquerque 87131
Art Dept.: MFA, Still Photography

New York

NEW YORK UNIVERSITY, 80 Washington Sq. E., New York 10003
Film—TV Dept.: MFA, Motion Pictures
PRATT INSTITUTE, 215 Ryerson, Brooklyn 11205
Photography Dept.: MFA, Still Photography
ROCHESTER INSTITUTE OF TECHNOLOGY, One Lomb Memorial Dr., Rochester 14623
Graphic Arts and Photography Dept.: MFA, Still Photography, Motion Pictures, and Graphic Arts

Ohio

OHIO UNIVERSITY, Athens 45701
Film Dept.: MFA, Motion Pictures
Photography Dept.: MFA, Still Photography

South Carolina

CLEMSON UNIVERSITY, Clemson 29631
History and Visual Studies Dept.: MFA, Still Photography

Utah

BRIGHAM YOUNG UNIVERSITY, Provo 84601
Communications and Art Dept.: MFA, Still Photography and Graphic Arts

Wisconsin

UNIVERSITY OF WISCONSIN, Madison 53706
Art Dept.: MFA, Still Photography and Graphic Arts

CANADA

UNIVERSITY OF ALBERTA, Edmonton, Alberta T6G0X7
Art and Design Dept.: MVA (Master of Visual Arts), Still Photography

Arizona

ARIZONA STATE UNIVERSITY, Tempe 85281
Graphic Communications Dept.: PhD, DEd, Graphic Arts

California

UNIVERSITY OF SOUTHERN CALIFORNIA, University Park, Los Angeles 90007
Cinema Dept.: PhD, Motion Pictures

Illinois

NORTHWESTERN UNIVERSITY, Evanston 60201

Radio—TV—Film Dept.: PhD, DEd, Motion Pictures

New Mexico

THE UNIVERSITY OF NEW MEXICO, Albuquerque 87131
Art Dept.: PhD, Still Photography

New York

NEW YORK UNIVERSITY, 80 Washington Sq. E., New York 10003
Art Education Dept.: PhD, DEd, Still Photography

Schools With Photography as a Primary Emphasis

California

ANSEL ADAMS YOSEMITE PHOTOGRAPHY WORKSHOP
Best's Studio, Box 455
Yosemite National Park 95389
JULIAN HIATT SCHOOL OF PHOTOGRAPHY
27-0 E. Pacific Coast Highway
Long Beach
THE GLEN FISHBACK SCHOOL OF PHOTOGRAPHY
3307 Broadway
Sacramento 95817
THE IMAGE CIRCLE, INC.
P.O. Box 9003
Berkeley 94909

Colorado

COLORADO PHOTOGRAPHIC ARTS CENTER
14900 Cactus Circle
Golden 80401
NATIONAL CAMERA TECHNICAL TRAINING DIVISION, INC.
2000 West Union Avenue
Englewood 80110

Connecticut

FAMOUS PHOTOGRAPHERS SCHOOL
Westport 06880

Florida

MIAMI PHOTOGRAPHY COLLEGE
1230 Ali Baba Avenue
Opa Locka 33054

Idaho

SUN VALLEY CENTER FOR THE ARTS
AND HUMANITIES
Box 1153
Sun Valley

Illinois

AMERICAN SCHOOL OF PHOTOGRAPHY
835 Diversey Parkway
Chicago 60614
RAY—VOGUE SCHOOLS
750 N. Michigan Avenue
Chicago 60611
WINONA SCHOOL OF PROFESSIONAL
PHOTOGRAPHY
Professional Photographers of
America, Inc.
1090 Executive Way
Des Plaines 60018

Kentucky

CENTER FOR PHOTOGRAPHIC STUDIES
131 W. Main Street
Louisville 40202
LEXINGTON PHOTOGRAPHY WORK-
SHOP
838 E. High Street
Lexington 40502

Massachusetts

IMAGEWORKS
63 Rogers Street
Cambridge 02142
WARREN STREET SCREEN PRESS
29 Warren Street
Cambridge 02141

Michigan

ART SCHOOL OF THE SOCIETY OF ARTS
AND CRAFTS
245 East Kirby
Detroit 48202
SARGENT ART SCHOOL
14309 West McNichols
Detroit 48235

Minnesota

MINNEAPOLIS AREA VOCATIONAL
SCHOOL

1101 Third Avenue S.
Minneapolis 55424
MINNEAPOLIS COLLEGE OF ART AND
DESIGN
200 East 25th Street
Minneapolis 55404

New York

APEIRON WORKSHOPS, INC.
Box 551
Millerton 12546
COLLEGE AT OLD WESTBURY
Planting Fields
Oyster Bay 11771
GERMAIN SCHOOL OF PHOTOGRAPHY
225 Broadway
New York 10007
NEW YORK INSTITUTE OF PHOTOGRA-
PHY
10 West 33rd Street
New York 10001

Ohio

OHIO INSTITUTE OF PHOTOGRAPHY
4435 East Patterson Road
Dayton 45430

Pennsylvania

ANTONELLI SCHOOL OF PHOTOGRA-
PHY AND LITHOGRAPHY
209 N. Broad Street
Philadelphia 19107
STUDIO SCHOOL OF ART AND DESIGN
1424 Spruce Street
Philadelphia 19102

Rhode Island

RHODE ISLAND SCHOOL OF PHOTOG-
RAPHY, INC.
241 Webster Avenue
Providence 02909

Texas

ELKINS INSTITUTE SCHOOL OF PHO-
TOGRAPHY
2711 Inwood Road
Dallas 75235

Vermont

DOSCHER COUNTRY SCHOOL OF PHO-
TOGRAPHY
Tory Hill
South Woodstock 05071

Washington State

VETERANS ADMINISTRATION HOSPI-
TAL
4435 Beacon Avenue S.
Seattle 98108

Wisconsin

COUNTRY PHOTOGRAPHY WORKSHOP
Box 83
Woodman 53827

CANADA

GALLERY OF PHOTOGRAPHY
61 Lonsdale
North Vancouver
British Columbia

INDEX

The Author

At age 25, *Amy Rennert* has progressed rapidly from her first journalism job writing obituaries and weather reports for the *Colorado Springs Sun*. Currently a resident of San Francisco, she is a contributing editor and consumer columnist for *New West*, a popular bi-weekly West Coast magazine. Her articles have appeared in several other publications including *Womens Sports* magazine, the *San Francisco Examiner*, the *San Francisco Chronicle*, the *Los Angeles Herald-Examiner* and the *San Mateo Times*. Ms. Rennert's interest in journalism is complemented by her interest and involvement in community and consumer affairs. *MAKING IT IN PHOTOGRAPHY* is her first book.

The Photographer

Bruce Curtis is a well-known photographer who travels the world on assignment for *Sports Illustrated, Time, Racquet,* and *Newsweek.* His assignments have included such diverse events as Richard Nixon's trip to China and Muhammed Ali's fight against Joe Frazier in Manila. Mr. Curtis has been a professional photographer since he was seventeen, when he covered the Algerian civil war. Primarily a photographer of sporting events, he has a permanent exhibition at the Tennis Hall of Fame, and is one of the few photographers in the United States to master the art of stroboscopic photography.

For Putnam's, Bruce Curtis is the photographer for *Steve Cauthen: Boy Jockey* by Anthony Tuttle, *Perfect Balance: The Story of an Elite Gymnast* by Lynn Haney, *The Great Game of Soccer* by Howard Liss, and *Tracy Austin: Tennis Wonder* by Peter Talbert.